The Stimulus Driven Brain

The Essential Guide for the ADD/ADHD College Student

George H. Glade
M.C., M.N., ARNP

5550 Angstrom Press, LLC

The Stimulus Driven Brain
The Essential Guide for the ADD/ADHD College Student
November 2009

ISBN 978-0-9843420-0-6

Cover design by Devan Register
Editor Kathryn Willemsen

5550 Angstrom Press, LLC
1800 Westlake Ave. N. Suite 303
Seattle, WA 98109

Printed in the United States.

This book is dedicated to Albert Reichert, M.D., a gifted healer, a role model for good practice, a wise mentor both personal and professional and someone I have been fortunate enough to call my friend.

Acknowledgements

Everyone needs a good editor and I have been fortunate in finding one in Kathryn Willemsen. We get too close to our work and lose the objectivity to see it as others will. Ms. Willemsen has pushed me to be better and to demand more of myself and what I write. This book is greatly improved as a result of her firm, direct feedback, and articulate guidance.

Devan Register is a brilliant, up and coming graphic designer. His cover design was more than I could have hoped for. He captured the essence of what I envisioned when I titled the book.

Thank you both.

Chapters

·1·
What is ADD/ADHD?

"The thing I lose patience with the most is the
clock. Its hands move too fast."
-*Thomas Edison*

"The mind is not a vessel to be filled, but a
fire to be kindled."
-*Plutarch*

Despite popular belief, ADD/ADHD is not a psychological problem, but a neurologically different type of brain. It is not caused by inadequate parenting or low socioeconomic status. The work of Daniel Amen, M.D. and others have demonstrated that the ADD/ADHD brain carried different level of key neurotransmitters (1). Patterns of activation and blood flow, particularly in the cerebral context are predictably different. The ADD brain is a stimulus driven brain. When given a stimulus that the individual finds interesting, focus can actually be quite good. However, with content that is uninteresting, the mind wanders. The individual focuses on the other thoughts.

It is unfortunate that primary education teachers are still not very good at identifying the stimulus pattern as a marker for ADD/ADHD. All too often, the students get labeled as stupid or lazy and they are said to "not apply" themselves, and unfortunately, this message will often be reinforced at home. Many people with ADD grapple with a self-concept formed by very negative and inaccurate messages. Report cards for children with ADD are full of comments like "Not working to full potential" or "Needs to apply themselves." Children may interrupt teachers and peers or have difficulty staying in their seats

While there are few studies which support this, boys tend to have more symptoms of hyperactivity that girls (2). When girls do have hyperactivity, it can be as severe or more severe than boys. Children and teens with hyperactivity appear restless and can't sit still in class. They can be irritable and get into fights often. They will make careless mistakes, and will lose things. This is truly the outer layer of the onion. Many serious learning problems can develop. An ADD brain can be marked by slower cognitive processing. Often times, motor coordination is poor, leading to sloppy handwriting. Working memory fails them, and memorization is quite difficult. There is often very slow retrieval of information, and the inability to express the information articulately. The experience for the ADD student can often be one of struggle because many have more difficulty putting words together, along with writing, and listening.

On the contrary, if a stimulus is particularly interesting to a student, that student will be attentive and focused when it is presented. Some people with ADD/ADHD are avid readers. On topics which are of interest, the child can do well in silent reading in class. If it's not a subject of interest, then the child may have trouble staying in their seat, or be day dreaming, their mind wandering. When students have this spotty presentation of doing well in some subjects (the ones they're interested in), and poorly on others, they get labeled as 'lazy.'

The real benefit of ADD/ADD is contained in marked differences in the way people are prone to think. For the person with a non-ADD/ADHD brain, they tend to be more adept at linear thinking. This thinking pattern is akin to a line of dominoes. Like dominoes, people who think in a linear manner think in terms of logical actions and consequences. They realize that in order to finish a project, it must be worked on consistently.

Yet, for the person with an ADD brain, thought processes can be much like throwing a rock into a still pool of water. People get a number of ideas that expand out, building upon one another. Sometimes this process is so rapid, it is akin to a firecracker going off in the air. Unfortunately, the fragments of paper fall to earth before the person can grab them, organize them, and put them into use. This plays out in a myriad of impractical ways. Take, for example, a person is taking the garbage out to the back alley to dump. He sees weeds that need to be pulled, and a neighbor shouts a "hello" while a stray cat run across his path. An assortment of small tasks and distractions become a diversion from completing the main task. For this ADD/ADHD person, a task that should've taken one or two minutes has suddenly been extended or completely forgotten.

The gift of this style of thinking is the ability to engage in what is best termed as synthesis thought. This means that people with synthesis thought take many different factors into consideration at once. This type of thinking is often the basis of creativity. ADD is a continuum, with some people having more profound difficulties with focus and attention than others. The ability to think creatively is a continuum as well. I know a number of other authors and people with ADD/ADHD are well represented in this occupation. There are many of occupations which are well suited to the abilities inherent in having a stimulus driven brain. These tend to be jobs which require the people to consider multiple factors concurrently and mesh these factors into solutions.

One of the best examples of creativity, and a stimulus driven mind is that of Thomas Edison. He was born to middle-class parents in Milan, Ohio. In 1847, this was one of the largest port cities in the United States. Thomas Edison's journey through formal education was at best a tumultuous period. His teacher had to contend with 38 students in a one-room schoolhouse. Mr. Edison was reported to be rather hyperactive, and his teacher made no attempt to hide their belief that he was "addled" and somehow defective, in his ability to learn. His mother wisely realized the failings of public education, and sought to teach young Thomas herself. He is reported to have started reading all of the books in his town's library. By age 12, he was said to of completed Gibbon's Rise and Fall of the Roman Empire, Burton's Anatomy of Melancholy, and Sear's History of the World. He had an insatiable thirst for science. He read the World Dictionary of Science and studied chemistry extensively. Not unlike many parents today when confronted by our own children's math homework, his own parents were unable to answer his questions about physics, such as those contained in Isaac Newton's Principia. They hired a tutor to help him digest and understand this work (3).

Edison had an insatiable mind, but also one which had a great degree of distractibility. In his lab in Menlo Park, he was able to create an environment where he could go from project to project.

His creativity resulted in more U.S. patents that any other single individual has been able to produce (3). He was able to turn his stimulus driven brain into a profound advantage.

We are surrounded by people that have the ability to think in this manner. If we look at the continuum of intelligence, we will find that a graph of the incidence of ADD/ADHD has two peaks. One is found with developmental disabilities. If we eliminate that part of the population, we find a distribution of ADD/ADHD is highly skewed to higher levels of intelligence. In my practice, I have treated 13 people with PhDs, three attorneys, and quite a number of people with Masters degrees. All of these people had that level of achievement prior to being diagnosed with ADD/ADHD. This struggle experienced by people with ADD/ADHD is a continuum as well. The people in my practice achieved a high level of academic accomplishment because they had the intellectual horsepower to do so. In a school environment, the expectations are laid out at the beginning of the quarter. Even the last minute papers can be evaluated quite positively given the intelligence to extrapolate from class material and other sources to come up with a paper. It's when the person enters the real world where they are deluged with changing demands and unforeseen expectations that raw intelligence fails to do the job. Entering college raises the bar of academic expectations and the old ways which got you by tend to not serve you as well.

John's Story

"I think I'm the original "the dog ate my homework guy." I've mastered so many excuses for why stuff doesn't get done that I feel like I'm kind of a fraud. In school, being polite and a likeable guy got me cut a lot of slack. I could hold my own in class room discussions. Profs like when you speak up. It's just thinking about the subject while you're talking about it. It's not because I ever did much of the reading. I'm a pretty slow reader so I had made the decision just to skim over most of that. Now I get lots of calls and can't seem to get anything done without interruption. It throws my off. It's not like I have a course outline to look at. Post-it notes are everywhere. Lots of times I will just sit at my desk, not doing anything about it."

For the person entering college, or finding that the bar has been raised much higher in graduate or professional school, there are unique challenges. Many of these challenges revolve around executive functioning or the cognitive abilities that control or regulate other abilities and behaviors. These functions are the basis for any goal-directed behavior. They allow us to stop and start actions. Think of them as a "wise watch dog" which monitors and changes behavior as needed. Executive functions allow us to plan for future new tasks and situations. They are the part of our cognitive functioning that anticipates what may happen and permits our adaptation to changing situations. We can form concepts and think abstractly. For the person with ADD/ADHD, executive functions are weaker than for people without an ADD/ADHD brain. It can be more difficult to hold events in one's mind. A dimension of abstraction involves taking a concept apart and reconstituting it. This can be a challenge when one is faced with distractibility and difficulties with focus.

Social autonomy for the college freshman may be a very new experience and present its own challenges. For the first time in one's life, the new student is accountable only for themselves. The amount of reading can rise to more than the length of a novel on a weekly basis. Professors aren't teaching toward the low middle of the population. They move faster and cover more material. The work load is drastically escalated. There is an expectation of a higher level of integration. While they might have stood out as potentially more capable then their peers, the new student is in an environment where everyone is bright and qualified to be in school.

Perhaps you're just starting out in your educational career. Maybe you've been at it for a while, and are tired of the struggle to keep pace with other students. Maybe you're going to enter graduate or professional school, and know that the demands are going to increase. Your education may sit side by side with the reality of having a family or a full or part-time job. You may have asked yourself, "How will I juggle school work and family?" I have personally encountered these very same struggles. When it comes to education, or many of life's tasks, often our response is to do more and work harder. The brute force approach of putting in an inordinate amount of hours will leave you exhausted. School should be not be a time where you feel utterly spent by the experience. You shouldn't feel like you've cheated yourself out of the enjoyable parts of going to school.

This book takes a holistic look at ADD/ADHD, and the challenges which face college student with ADD/ADHD. It contains both study skills and different ways of taking on a raised bar of expectations found in college. Our sense of our capabilities is influenced by what we believe about ourselves. Beliefs can be yet another barrier to success in college. This book will help you examine and challenges these beliefs. If your ADD/ADHD is just coming to light now that you've entered college, it will give you information regarding medications and what to look for in looking for a provider to prescribe those medications. We all live in a social context. Maintaining relationships is an important part of a successful college experience. I've long held a belief about school and life: If you lose what is most important to you, you have not succeeded. It doesn't matter what letters you'll be able to put behind your name.

·2·
The Power of Beliefs

"There is nothing either good or bad, but thinking makes it so."
-William Shakespeare

John Wont of the Curaco jazz band Blue Apple Trio expressed the power of belief quite clearly. "We are who we believe ourselves to be." If we have the belief that we will be successful, our odds of achievement increase. If we believe we cannot accomplish something, then our chances of succeeding decrease. Our beliefs start early in life. If you talk to a class of children in kindergarten, and you asked them all "Who would like to go on a 50 mile hike right now?" Most, if not all of the hands and the class would shoot up, eager to go. There would be no belief in failure. If you asked the same question of children in middle school or adolescents in high school, progressively fewer hands would go up. If you asked a group of adults, most would look at you as if you were crazy. At best, one or two hands might be raised.

Formal education can sometimes stifle belief and creativity. One of my earliest memories is of an art teacher telling me that cows could be black, brown or white, not purple after I had drawn a purple cow. What would the world have lost if Picasso had followed those rules? This is but one aspect of the formation of beliefs. For the student who does very well in subjects that meets the interest of his/her stimulus driven brain, but does poorly in less interesting courses, the label all too often is that he/she is lazy or even stupid. For many people with ADD/ADHD, there is a succession of negative messages that lead to a lack of self confidence, and a loss of a sense of personal power. Sometimes, a teacher or parent's feedback, although seemingly insignificant, has a lasting place in our memory and contributes to our belief about ourselves. To this day I recall what the art teacher said about what a cow could or couldn't be, even though it has been many years since that occurred.

What do we feel when somebody says: "That's a really tough course," or perhaps "Professor Johnson is really hard." How we describe things are windows to our thoughts and often our internal dialogue about those challenges. How is it different when someone tells us that that a course in school was one of the best they had ever had? We look forward to taking that course ourselves. We have a response set about our experience in that course. All these are descriptive phrases. They are precise representations of what is going on in our mind. How we frame things can connect this back to our previous experience, during times of struggle, and periods where our sense of our own resources were at a low point.

Thinking in the negative puts us in the negative state. Self-talk can amplify, and can become a persistent inner dialogue that reflects the belief. These beliefs have a behavioral outcome. This relationship was made very clear, by Richard Ellis, a psychologist, who formulated a therapeutic paradigm called Rational Emotive Therapy (RET).

Let's place two people under exactly the same circumstances. The situation doesn't matter. This 'Activating Event' leads to some sort of reaction that is different for each of the two individuals. It leads to a 'Consequence.' This can be emotional, physical or behavioral. If two people are laid off from work, one might think that the activating event is a terrible thing. It might assault their sense of who they are. Another person might see that as opportunity. A bit of time off, getting unemployment insurance is just the thing to allow them to look for a better job, where they might be more satisfied, and potentially make more money. What separates the two individuals' reaction or 'Consequence' is what they believe about the situation.

We arrive in adulthood having a sense of identity that begins to crystallize in our late teens to mid 20s. During this period of our life span, our developmental task is the formation of our sense of self. If our life in late adolescence and early adulthood is a time of struggle, our sense of who we are becomes based on that experience. Fortunately, self perception is not carved in stone. A variety of cognitive-behavioral therapies provide ways of challenging thinking about the beliefs we carry into adulthood. We have many ways of thinking, which in the variety of cognitive therapies are called cognitive distortions. These are inaccurate thoughts or ideas which serve to support negative thinking and the emotions which grow out of our thoughts. They are fallacies of logic. When we challenge these negative thoughts often we can eliminate a sense of feeling depressed or anxious. The process of learning to challenge and refute these ideas is called "cognitive restructuring" (1).

Let's consider some of the ways beliefs may get in your way and lead to negative feelings I want you to take recent incidents in your life that have resulted in a strong emotional reaction. These could be items that you inherently resist thinking about. If your internal dialogue begins with "I couldn't possibly..." then this is an area that really suggests a strong belief system. Recognizing cognitive distortions is a fairly easy task when you know what to cue on. They cause painful emotions such as depression, anxiety, worry, and avoidance of particular things. Sometimes they lead you to have ongoing conflict with other people in your life. For the person with ADD/ADHD, they can be a very real barrier to achieving our fullest potential.

Examples of Cognitive Distortion

Selective Attention
This filtering occurs when we look at only one part of the situation to the exclusion of everything else.

Example: The ADD/ADHD person may have a tendency to look at just the negatives in a situation. An all too common experience is for a teacher to call on an ADD person, and instead of paying attention, the student's mind was wandering. They may have momentarily lost track of the discussion or just may not know the answer. They don't realize that they may not be the only one who doesn't know the answer. The student may have felt exquisitely uncomfortable during that moment. It may carry them back to similar experiences.

Distorted perception: "I have to always know the answer. If I don't, then I'll stand out as less able and not as smart as others. I can't enjoy this class unless I'm more on top of things all of the time."

Rational Dispute: "There are lots of times I make a solid contribution to the discussion. Other students all have times where they may not have the answer. I can take control of my negative feeling by being well prepared before I come to class."

Polarized or Black and White Thinking

This type of thinking leads to only 'either-or' option and is classic black or white thinking. There is no middle ground. The focus remains only on extremes. Most things in life exist on a continuum rather than two mutually exclusive parts. It is not uncommon for people with this type of thinking have problems with mood swings. This is not depression. Depression is a more sustained phenomenon. This is best described as emotional dysregulation where internal dialogue leads to feeling bad. It is easily confused with depression. It is a hallmark of the perfectionist. It is the foundation to the belief that I am either all good or I am a failure. The difficulty for the perfectionist is that it one can never quite be good enough. The bar just keeps moving higher.

Example: I only got a B+ on the history test. I'll never make it into law school. I am a failure.

Distorted Perception: My academic performance defines my personal worth as a human being. This one grade will determine the course of my life.

Rational Dispute: Getting a B + is not a bad grade at all. I worked hard for that, and I did my best. I feel I came away with a good level of knowledge about the subject.

It's Always Going to be That Way

This is an easy trap for people with ADD/ADHD to fall into if they have had more of an academic struggle. It is the caveat to the notion that the best predictor to current performance is past performance.

They over generalize in thinking that they can never be successful at school because they never have been successful. When I first work with a person with this type of history on medications, I tell them that this is a time to challenge their previous notions about what they are capable of doing. I have had numbers of people tell me they didn't realize that they actually were smart. It often starts slowly with dipping just a toe into the academic waters by taking a single class at community college. They do better than they expected, often very well. Momentum builds and they increase the degree of challenge. It is enormously gratifying to play a small role in this process of growth.

Example: I've just got a 'good enough degree' (GED). What makes me think I've got the ability to go to college?

Distorted Perception: I've always struggled with school and I always will.

Rational Dispute: I've figured out that I have a challenge to my ability to learn that can be modified. It's time to figure out what I'm really capable of.

I Know What You're Thinking

Actions are linked to the erroneous belief that somehow we can actually read other people's mind. In this case, you base your assumptions and conclusions on your ability to' know' other people's thoughts. People with ADD/ADHD can have a tendency to talk over others because they have anticipated what the person is going to say. Their mind is jumping ahead in the conversation, weighing various aspects of what is being said. Blurting out statements is not unusual. Misreading conversations or intentions if often times the result.

Example: He didn't say anything about my paper. I know that he doesn't like it. He is going to think I don't know what I'm doing.

Distorted Perception: "I know what he is thinking when he looked at me."

Rational Dispute: Only the person themselves knows what they are thinking about. If I'm not sure about their reaction, I can ask them what they think. Maybe he hasn't read my paper or is trying to separate mine from everyone else's.

Chicken Little Syndrome

It's a catastrophe! Certainly the end of the world must be near. People with ADD/ADHD certainly do not have this market cornered. It is an equal opportunity cognitive distortion. When the lead domino in the line is tipped over, a succession of irrational thoughts follow leading to an endpoint of the worst case scenario. There is the expectation that things will be the worst, often times it becomes one of those self-fulfilling prophecies. Our expectations affect the outcome of situations.

Example: "I'm not going to get my paper in on time, now I'm going to fail the class. I will have to repeat this course and it is only offered once a year. I'm not going to graduate on time. My parents are going to kill me. They won't help me financially with school anymore. I'll wind up working n fast food for the rest of my life." (Okay, I've over dramatized this a bit. For the person who winds up thinking catastrophically, it can seem like the end of the world.)

Distorted Perception: One paper determines my whole academic career.

Rational Dispute: I can talk to the professor about needing more time. Perhaps I can negotiate getting more time, even if it means a slightly lower grade. This is but one paper among many I'll write while I'm at college. When I'm in the work world, no one will ever ask what grades I got when I was in college.

It's All my Fault

For the person with ADD/ADHD, who has developed many negative perceptions about themselves, everything in the world is interpreted in a way that reflects negative self concept. This cognitive distortion incorporates facets of other distortions such as filtering out the positives. It is a polarized way of thinking that lends itself to an all or nothing view of one's self and one's abilities. The outcome is that the world is seen through a lens of negative beliefs. The explanation is interpreted as being caused by what the person views as their failings as a person.

Example: "If only I were... (smarter, thinner, prettier, taller, more athletic, etc,) then I'd be...

Distorted Perception: I'm just this way and I can't change it or do things as a result of being this way.

Rational Dispute: Who I am is not etched in stone. I can take on new information and make changes in my life.

It's Just Not Fair

The fallacy of fairness is a common trap that many of us fall into. We judge people's actions by the rules we've determined are right or wrong. The difficulty is that in personal interactions, everyone has different ideas about what is fair. Sometimes this grows out of sense of entitlement. Reality check: we're no more or less special than anyone else. We don't "deserve" to be treated better than others because of who we are or what we contend with. This perception does not take into account other people's needs.

Example: It's not fair that the school won't grant me accommodations to assist me in overcoming my difficulties with ADD.

Distorted Perception: This is a dangerous distortion for the ADD person. It suggests that ADD has become a way of self definition. There is an egocentric distortion with this particular example that concludes that one is somehow special and others should treat you differently because you 'deserve' it.

Rational Dispute: I'm getting as good a grade as others in the class. ADD is a challenge I have to contend with but my performance doesn't support the need to have accommodations.

I Feel This Way That Must Be How It Is

This is the distorted belief that everything you feel must be true. It leads one to jump to a conclusion, based on initial reaction, or an ongoing belief system, which causes us to struggle. The ADD/ADHD person can easily incorporate the overt and covert negative messages that grew from others perceptions of our school or social performance. For the child growing up with a stimulus driven brain, it is very common to do well in subjects that are of interest while having dismal performance in classes that are uninteresting. All too often, kids get labeled lazy or stupid. These are the messages that crush self confidence.

Example: I feel stupid when I tried math problems, therefore I must be stupid.

Distorted Perceptions: Subjective feelings ALWAYS reflect reality. This example is a permutation of over generalizing.

Rational Dispute: I'm talented in a lot of ways that unfortunately doesn't include math. In fact, I hate math. It doesn't appeal to me at all. I am, however, really good at art, science and history.

It's All Your Fault

This is a very common distortion and is exactly what it sounds like: bad things happen and it's someone else who is at fault. The confusing part of it is that sometimes things happen that truly are out of our control and as result of others behavior. Our externalized blaming can sometime include attributing human characteristics to inanimate objects. An example might be telling yourself the car 'refused' to start, as if the vehicle made a choice regarding wanting to start or not.

Example: My family was so messed up, how could I have possibly figured out how to have a good relationship?

Distorted Perception: Having a dysfunctional family means I too need to follow that script of dysfunction in my own life.

Rational Dispute: I don't need to be the person, or have the behaviors that my family does. I can explore an assortment of different ways of coping.

The Little Dictator of "I Should"

'I Should' is a tyrant that dwells in our mind. It is an implied obligation. It operates as a rigid set of indisputable rules about how we should be in our life.

Example: I should never get angry.

Distorted Perception: Anger is a destructive force. Anger is inherently bad.

Rational Dispute: I have a wide range of emotions, just like everyone else. Anger is just one of them. Anger, properly focused can result in the setting appropriate and assertive boundaries for myself.

Exercise

This strategy was developed by Albert Ellis, MD, the creator of Ration Emotive Therapy, one of the cognitive behavioral paradigms (2). Dr. Ellis was a prolific writer, theorist and therapist who passed away in 2007. His work has been used by therapist for the past thirty years. I would suggest you take a separate piece of paper and follow this paradigm of thought.

1. Describe an event in your life where you have a strong emotional reaction to that event. (Activating Event).
2. What did you do? What was your emotional state as a result of this? How do you wish this had gone differently? (Consequence).
3. What was the belief system that was operating here? Did you have a sense that your perceptions are skewed or in some way distorted? (Belief).
4. How have you observed other people reacting to the same set of circumstances? How would you have liked to experience the event differently? What are different beliefs that would account for other people reacting in different ways? Brainstorm potential alternative beliefs, and write down how they may have led to a different emotional or behavioral consequence. (Refute the belief).

Balance in Our Self Perceptions

It is not uncommon for people who received treatment as an adult to have incorporated many of the more negative messages, both overt and covert into their sense of who they are. Suddenly there struggles have both a name and an explanation. The map is not the territory. ADD/ADHD is not who we are. Yes, it is a challenge. Though it can lead to difficulties, it can be the fuel of marvelous creativity and passion.

What form should treatment take? Having ADD/ADHD is not something you have to treat as a means of preserving life. Taking medications is often viewed from a medical model perspective of treating pathology: that there is something wrong that needs to be changed. This enters into our self perception. Many people look differently on medications that work in the brain as different that one's that work elsewhere in the body. This is yet another dimension of how taking medication can affect our self perception. Medications can bring profound benefits into people's lives. I believe they are best viewed as a tool and are complemented by other interventions. Coaching, exercise and change in diet all have a beneficial roll in addressing ADD/ADHD.

Thom Harman, is a former psychotherapist, talk show host, liberal political commentator and entrepreneur. He has written some very good books about ADD/ADHD, proposes a model, which conceptualizes people as Hunters or Farmer's, each with their unique characteristics (3). He discusses the struggle of a hunter in a farmer's world. He takes up the complex question of medications. While he notes the use of medications are not incompatible for the hunter (person with ADD/ADHD), he makes the point that medications change people in negative ways and rob them of the aspects of ADD that are of benefit. He implies that the very things that make a person creative, flexible and able to take risks are erased by the use of medications. My own experience treating people with ADD/ADHD is very much the opposite. At some point you will likely have to make your own decision about this.

Catherine's Perspective

This is a letter of a woman I see who makes her living as a professional artist. She generously provided this letter, which I have included because it speaks to the concern that a part of them will be lost with treatment on medication

I was 52 when I was diagnosed with ADD. It's not like I hadn't spent the last 25 years (not to mention a small fortune) in various therapies, anti-depressants, etc. in a continuous effort to figure out what was "wrong with me." Imagine my chagrin when I was told that, within 20-40 minutes I would feel the effects of my medication and the obvious difference they would make.

In retrospect, it makes perfect sense that I became an abstract painter. (Thank God I live in the 20th century and went to a school where such behavior is not only acceptable it's respected.) Painting served as my translator in life. I had always felt the need for visual aids as words turned into alphabet soup in my brain.

The change that occurred in regards to my work was huge:

1. I have more energy
2. I was able to organize my studio so that it was supportive versus oppressive
3. My work is not so existential/not required to validate or "work for me"
4. It doesn't matter if I get it "right"
5. I can do things for the hell of it or fun of it or just to see what happens
6. The final outcome of my work is less important than the adventure
7. I'm no longer expecting a child to fulfill my requirements.
8. I am more able to feed my desires rather than my "needs"
9. I can do whatever I want (WHAT?)!

Now I am less a victim of circumstances- if I don't like something I simply change it and move on. Now, rather than being stuck I cut straight to the chase.

I feel like my electrical cord has been plugged in, and I have been promoted to an executive position. I SAIL THE BOAT. I'm not a passenger in steerage.

As a result, my studio is less of a battle field and less of a fight for survival. I don't dread the studio and feel sick to my stomach.

The best part is that I recognize my paintings as friends, and I don't start from scratch each day. I can pick up where I left off and remember what I know. Now that I know my own mind and have my own voice my art is free to be itself.

Needless to say this is more than a bit overwhelming. Apparently I've been saving all of this up for some time. I'm still the same person, neurosis still intact fears, etc. I can still procrastinate with the best of them, but I might mop the floor in the meantime. The hard artistic decisions are just as hard but you get to focus on THEM. It's way more fun that way. Now my paintings and I are on the same side.

And, if all else fails, I can rest assured that after 10-12 hours the spell wears off.

–Catherine.

Many clinicians will either regard ADD/ADHD as a disability, or is something that simply does not exist. If you view it as a disability, you will subtly act as if you're a person who is disabled. ADD ADHD is a phenomena characterized in a variety of ways. It's not an excuse for behavior.

There are many areas in the medical profession that focus on an illness model. The DSM-IV-TR, the manual for diagnosis of mental disorders identifies ADD/ADHD as a 'disorder' rather than a natural, genetically transmitted brain variation (4). Thomas Edison was labeled a mental defective in his youth. He was lucky that he had a mother who removed him from an environment which very well could have robbed him of any sense of self confidence. He was able to play to his strengths and utilize his stimulus driven brain to its fullest extent. Sitting at a desk, doing repetitive tasks is something that is unlikely to ever be a good fit for the person with a stimulus drive brain. It is interesting that in my practice, I have clusters of people in various occupations where they clearly have found work which fits for their stimulus driven brain (construction managers, athletes and trainers, and entrepreneurs).

I can say as a clinician who does utilize medications, that first and foremost, they are a tool. They are not the whole answer, and are best complemented by coaching or even psychotherapy. They are not necessarily for everyone. I disagree with Thom Hartman's contention that being on medication limits creativity or removes the urge of the hunter to hunt. I have a client who is a teacher. During summer vacations, he writes screenplays. In his first summer of being on medications, he was able to complete a screenplay, from the start: editing, rewriting and ultimately finishing the screenplay. This was the first time he had been able to accomplish this endeavor in such a short period of time. He never lacked the ability to write well and create. Medications were like taking all the horses that he had to run with, and putting them in the same harness. It is not a perspective of creativity lost, but of creativity harnessed, and directed.

This is one aspect of your making sense and putting your ADD/ADHD into perspective. I encourage you first and foremost, to get information from a wide variety of sources. Accept your power to make your own decisions, based on what you think, and your own conclusions. Whatever you decide about medications and other interventions you may wish to make on your ADD/ADHD, have it based on lots of information from multiple sources.

·3·
What You Should Know About Medication Providers and Initial Assessment

"It is better to know some of the questions than all of the answers."
-James Thurber

One thing to realize is that everybody, absolutely everybody has some of the signs and symptoms of ADD/ADHD. Everyone forgets things from time to time. We all have projects we don't complete. It is a universal fact that there will always be time that we find our thoughts distracted by things around us. You may have taken an online test. The questions may have jumped out at you and left you saying to yourself. "This is me we're talking about." One caution about online tests, it is more often than not, they are not rigorously standardized against a large number of subjects. None of the online tests will be viewed as valid if you need accommodations for school or formal testing procedures. At best, they give an indication to look further.

Many of the ADD/ADHD associations have a list of qualified providers. There are two, and in some states three types of providers that have the ability to prescribe medications. The first category is physicians. They have undergone four years of medical school, followed by a four-year residency. Many physicians, after their residency, will get more specialized training in the field in the form of a fellowship. These are generally between one and two years.

While every physician can prescribe medications for ADD/ADHD, my own belief and experience is that the physician needs specific training in treatment of ADD/ADHD. This is not necessarily your primary care provider, although many such physicians will prescribe stimulant medications. The expertise with which they do prescribe is highly variable. I have seen excellent work, and grossly inadequate work come at the hands of general practitioners. Many have not taken the time needed to assess if there might be other psychiatric conditions present. These are known as "co-morbidities. This specific expertise is more frequently found with physicians trained as psychiatrists. There are some neurologists that do ADD work, but they are uncommon.

The next category of providers are nurse practitioners. Nurse practitioners will have a Masters degree in Nursing. In a few years, the level of entry to become a nurse practitioner will be a Doctorate in Philosophy (PhD). Beyond their educational preparation, they have posts-graduate supervision hours that they need to complete, prior to taking a board examination. Nurse practitioners practice only in the field of their study. There can be considerable crossover with this. State laws will generally allow a person to diverge from their practice, if they have suitable training and study in a particular area. One might see a person who is prepared as a Family Nurse Practitioner, practicing in general psychiatry.

There has been a growing movement for quite a number of years to have psychologists prescribe. In addition to a doctoral level preparation and psychology, psychologists undergo additional formal education and supervision to be able to prescribe medications. At this point in time, prescribing psychologists are a minority. Many people debate the pros and cons of psychologist prescribing medications. The argument against their practice is that they lack the depth of knowledge in physiological functioning that both physicians and nurse practitioners have.

The best stance for physicians (even if they are psychiatrists, nurse practitioners, and prescribing psychologists) is to know clearly what their expertise is, and if that is not part of their preparation, hand off to someone who specializes in this type of work. Ask how many people they treat for ADD/ADHD and what percentage of their practice consists of ADD clients. Find out how long they have been doing this specialized work. I like people to take the perspective that they are interviewing a provider for the best fit for their needs.

In looking for a clinician to do medication work, it is important that you ask about their specific preparation to treat ADD/ADHD. A reasonable question is whether they provide counseling or coaching services as well. Some will provide these services and you can find everything you need with one person. If a clinician doesn't provide coaching, generally they will know clinicians who do. These may range widely in their academic preparation. Coaches range from people who have completed a specialized training program to coach people with ADD/ADHD to people with any of a variety of doctoral degrees. Does more education automatically make for a better coach? Not necessarily. I have encountered some extraordinarily talented coaches that have been through a specialized training program.

Co-morbidities

ADD/ADHD has a number of other diagnosable disorders that can occur with it. These are called co-morbidities. The presence of another disorder can confound a diagnosis of ADD ADHD. People with ADD/ADHD will often have much higher rates of co-morbid mental health conditions than found in the general population. In a recent National Co-morbidity Survey Replication, it was found that adults between the ages of 18-44 with ADD/ADHD had higher rates of major depressive disorder. Depression at this level was founded in 18.6% versus 7.8% founded in the general population. The numbers are also similar for bipolarity spectrum disorders. 19.4% of people of ADD/ADHD had bipolarity spectrum disorders as opposed to 3.1% in the general population. Anxiety disorders tend to increase with age. This is particularly true with ADD/ADHD. This survey found a frequency of anxiety disorders at 47.1% versus 19.5% for non--ADD/ADHD adults (1).

Many symptoms of mental health disorders overlap with the inattentive or restless symptoms of ADD/ADHD. When depression, bipolar disorder, or anxiety is well treated, it is easier to identify the person with ADD/ADHD. If the pronounced symptoms of depression, bipolarity or anxiety are treated, then the individual's day-to-day functioning becomes clearer.

There is no evidence-based guideline for treatment of ADD in the context of depression, bipolarity, or anxiety disorders. A starting point is to treat the condition that is considered to be most impairing first. For example, Dysthymia is a lower level of depression. More often than not, individuals with Dysthymia can go about their daily lives. They live in a flat, gray world. With the predominant treatment for ADD/ADHD being stimulants, one might look at treating the ADD first. The very earliest treatments for depression were stimulants. There is a possibility that use of the stimulant will effectively treat this lower level of depression.

When one looks at a person with a major depressive episode, you have to consider the degree of acuity and impairment. Depression has a significant mortality associated with it. Treating the depression first is the best course.

Bipolarity spectrum disorders have significant overlap with ADHD. Treating these two disorders when they occur at the same time, will require more than one medication. The choices for combined treatment includes psycho-stimulants and a mood stabilizer; psycho-stimulants and an atypical antipsychotic or psycho-stimulants and a mood stabilizer and an atypical antipsychotic. This is a case where bipolarity needs to be stabilized first. Ideally, one can find a clinician, who is experienced in treating both bipolarity and ADD/ADHD. My own belief is the complexity of this treatment should not be in the hands of people with a generalist or primary care practice.

Substance abuse disorders are quite common with ADD/ADHD. While clinicians vary widely in their perspective of treatment of ADD with co-morbid substance-abuse, it is generally not recommended to use stimulants because of an elevated risk of continued substance abuse. However, a more balanced view is coming into practice. Some inpatient chemical dependency treatment programs advise people to stay on stimulant meds if they have been appropriately diagnosed for ADD/ADHD. Individuals I have treated with co-morbid substance use disorders have consistently found that treatment of their ADD/ADHD is a significant benefit in achieving a comfortable sobriety.

Nicotine has been called the most addictive substance on the planet. It is interesting that some of the medications in a development phase are nicotine-based. The dangers of smoking are well-known, and need not be elaborated here. For the person with ADD/ADHD, nicotine is reinforcing beyond its well-known addictive potential smoking and psychological ability to reduce anxiety. Most people whether they have ADD/ADHD or not say that they smoke as a stress reliever. With anxiety, or really getting stressed about something, often the first coping with that is to reach for cigarette. The irony is that cigarettes actually increase stress levels. When you look at the physiology of smoking, it mirrors all of the signs and symptoms of increase stress. Blood pressure goes up and heart rate increases. The sense of relieving stress is a conditioned response, with just the smell and feel of a cigarette telling your brain to relax. As your brain relaxes your body, it creates the illusion that your body is actually relaxed. There have been a number of studies that point to maternal smoking during pregnancy as suspected to be associated with ADD symptoms in children. The confounding feature to the studies is that there are a variety of lifestyle factors which may also be associated with development of ADD/ADHD. Smoking has always been associated with a wide array of infant health complications. Smoking cessation is difficult at best. In my clinical experience, people found quitting smoking easier once their ADD/ADHD was treated.

Short acting stimulants have a high risk of abuse. I have experienced these prescribed as a first-line by clinicians who do not specialize in this treatment. Longer acting medication has a far lower potential for abuse. They lack the quick onset found in short acting agents. In recent clinical trials for a methamphetamine preparation, the medication was evaluated by people with active addictions for its abuse potential. On a 25 point scale, long-acting agents were rated as a one or two. This is compared to substances such as cocaine, which will be rated as 20 or more. An alternative exists for treatment of people with substance abuse in at atomoxetine, a non-stimulant medication used in treatment of ADD/ADHD (3).

All treatment begins with good solid assessment. The average time for a visit with a primary care physician is in the range of eight to 12 minutes (2). This tends to be somewhat longer for nurse practitioners engaged in primary care. A skillful job of differential diagnosis, takes time even for a very experienced clinician. Even with taking somewhat longer, in a primary care setting, the risk of missing important co-morbidities is there. Missing key features of a person's presentation, pure and simple, increases the risk of bad outcomes. My own belief and approach incorporates a great deal of education about ADD/ADHD, and what we can expect from medications, and a reasonable timeline for these expectations. There are a number of scales available to clinicians which are statistically validated, by testing large numbers of individuals.

Prudent providers rely on not just interviews but they also formally test individuals for ADD/ADHD. The Diagnostic and Statistical Manual-IV (DSM-IV) remains the gold standard for diagnosis of ADD/ADHD. Assessment using the DSM-IV is by interview. In addition to a diagnostic interview, formal testing should be utilized. This gives an objective measure of the presence of ADD/ADHD and what sub-type a person may have. Some of the more common testing instruments for assessing ADD/ADHD are:

Brown Attention Deficit Disorder Scales

Connors Adult Attention Deficit Scale

DuPaul ADD/ ADHD Rating Scale

Wender Utah Rating Scale

All of these assessment tests will be satisfactory for validating academic accommodations. If you and the clinician plan to petition for academic accommodations, having recognized and statistically validated testing is a necessary part of the accommodation petition.

·4·
What You Should Know and Understand About Medications

"If we value the pursuit of knowledge, we must be
free to follow wherever that search may lead us.
The free mind is not a barking dog, to be tethered
on a 10 foot chain."
-Adlai E. Stevenson, Jr.

Many people have an anti-medication perspective. When they hear that one of the main types of stimulant is a methamphetamine molecule, the association with 'street meth' is understandable and evokes visions of being drug dependent. The fundamental differences lie in dose (milligrams vs. grams with methamphetamine abuse) and the fact that the molecule found in medications is a pharmacological standard. The irony is that treating ADD/ADHD can reduce the likelihood of chemical dependency problems with girls and bring it to a point where it is on a par with non-ADD males.

People also worry about not feeling like themselves and that they will be emotionally blunted. This is a marker that suggests the person is on the wrong class of medications. A skilled provider should ask about this nuance of a response. Some of my therapy clients have made the suggestion that 'insight' is a possible side effect. Many others note profound changes in their sense of being in the world.

Stimulants represent the first line of treatment for people with ADD/ADHD. There is also a non-stimulant and antidepressant preparations in current use. When compared to the effectiveness of stimulants, these are second tier choices.

A variety of neurotransmitters are responsible for higher brain functions. They are the signalers for a wide variety of emotional states. They are implicated in an array of psychiatric illnesses. The medications used to address these function by regulating the availability of an assortment of neurotransmitters. They play a role in decision making, control of our impulses, motor integration and memory. While an in depth discussion of neurotransmitter activity is beyond the scope of this book, stimulates affect neurotransmitter activity in the brain leading to the changes in both brain physiology and activity (1).

There are two types or classes of stimulants available. They are the methylphenidates (MPH) and the methamphetamine salts (MAS). They both affect the same parts of the brain, albeit with slightly different biochemical pathways. What determines which class of medication is better for an individual is a matter of both toleration and response. Poor reactions to medications are often due to the fact they have not been on the right medication. Generally switching the class of medication will address problems with toleration. There are people who don't tolerate either class of stimulant. It happens but fortunately, lack of toleration is an infrequent occurrence.

Strattera (atomoxetine) is a non-stimulant preparation for treatment of ADD/ADHD. It provides 24 hour coverage with a single daily dose. It takes six to eight weeks to evaluate response as contrasted to the stimulants where you figure out the best class and best dose in several weeks. Relative to stimulants, this particular medication does not have the efficacy or tolerability that stimulants do. While it is generic in other countries, the US Patent does not expire until 2017.

The use of stimulants has a 90 year history. Stimulant medications were used as the first medications to treat depression. They are still used as an augmentation for mainline antidepressants, particularly refractory or treatment resistant depression, in addition their use in treating ADD/ADHD. While every medication has its own unique set of side effects, the side effect profile for both methamphetamine salts and methylphenidates is very similar. These can consist of appetite suppression, weight loss, sleep disturbance, anxiety, and increase in obsessive behavior or tics.

Methamphetamine salts have two preparations currently available. Methylphenidates are the older class of medications, and there are significantly more preparations available. The following is a brief overview of these medications.

Methamphetamine Salts

Adderall XR. This medication contains equal amounts of four different amphetamine salts. The medication is encapsulated into two sets of coated beads that are pH activated as the medication travels through the gut. There are two release points for the medication. Given differences in individuals gastric pH, and G.I. transit time, there can be considerable variability between different people, in terms of the durability of response. On a practical basis, this can range from four to 10 hours. Another advantage of this preparation is, there are six dose increments, ranging from 5 mg to 30 mg. This allows for a great deal of flexibility in dosing. Adderall XR became available as a generic in the spring of 2009.

Adderall has a non-long-acting preparation as well. It consists of the same mix of four different amphetamine salts. The duration of response on this preparation can be 2-6 hours. An advantage is, this is available as a generic preparation. A disadvantage is that this has a much higher potential for abuse. Short acting medications have a very rapid onset of effect. It is this rapid effect that people with addiction problems seek. People may abuse this preparation of medication by snorting it or injecting it, in addition to taking large amounts.

In February of 2005, the US Food and Drug Administration issued a Public Health Advisory for Adderall and Adderall XR. Health Canada had suspended the sale of Adderall XR in the Canadian market. This was based on US reports of sudden deaths in pediatric patients. However, only a total of 12 cases were found. Five had occurred in patients with an underlying structural heart defect (abnormal arteries, abnormally thickened heart walls). These were all conditions that increase the risk for sudden death. Of the remaining cases, there were some problems with interpretation. These included family histories of ventricular tachycardia, association of death with heat exhaustion, dehydration and near drowning, very rigorous exercise, fatty liver, heart attacks and Type 1 diabetes mellitus. Treatment varied from one day to eight years.

The American FDA took a position of not taking any further regulatory action. They noted that when one considered the rate of sudden death in pediatric patients treated with Adderall, based on approximately 30 million prescriptions written between 1999 and 2003 (the period of time for these deaths occurred), the number of sudden deaths, was equivalent to what one would expect in the general population without any treatment.

Vyvanse (Lisdexamphetamine). This is a fairly new preparation/ delivery system, containing one amphetamine salt: Lisdexamphetamine, which has been in clinical use since 1939. The medication is what is called a "Prodrug". The molecule is therapeutically inactive until it is converted to its active form by metabolic processes. The amphetamine salt molecule is bonded with an amino acid molecule, l-lysine. When the medication enters into the G.I. tract, an enzyme cleaves the bond releasing active d-amphetamine. The advantage of this particular medication is often the duration of response is quite long. When this was in clinical trials, it was tested on children and adolescents. They found the effects as measured by the ability to do homework, sustained into the evening. This medication was available in the summer of 2007. It has a very smooth onset and period where effect drops off. Current research has determined that the effect on focus can last up to fourteen hours (2). This is ideal for the ADD/ADHD college student given the need for an extended number of hours where they will benefit from having focus improved.

Methylphenidates

There are many more choices in this category than for the MAS group. Many of these preparations have a short acting counterpart, which may be generic. The long-acting medications are as follows:

Daytrana Patch. The advancements for treatment of ADD/ADHD in the last 10 years have largely been due to advancements in the delivery system for these medications. This is true for the Daytrana patch, and is the first delivery system where the medication goes through the skin, rather than being absorbed by the G.I. tract. The medication releases a consistent amount of medication for as long as it is worn. The advantage of this is very long lasting coverage that is entirely smooth and consistent. Once the correct dose is found, the medication will be delivered until the person removes the patch. One dilemma is found if a person forgets to remove the patch. The medication will continue to be absorbed into the system. The side effect profile will remain the same, and often times it can disturb sleep. A practical disadvantage for men, as opposed to women is increased body hair. This reduces the number of sites available, where the patch can be placed. True skin rashes are rare. The skin irritation can be similar to wearing a Band-Aid for an extended period of time. Generally, this will resolve fairly quickly. There is some concern with the shelf life of the patch. I have had patients report to me, that when stored for several months, the patches do not seem as effective at the same dose. If a person is a methylphenidate best responder, this is a very good solution in a context where a person needs many hours of smooth coverage. College student are a prime example of people with this need.

Concerta is an extended release form of methylphenidate. The capsules are designed with a hydrating sponge mechanism that pushes the medication from the capsule. The capsule will pass with the stool. This too is an innovation in delivery system. The main factor in variability of response is G.I. transit time. Generally people will experience between 8-12 hours of coverage.

Metadate is another extended-release methylphenidate, which uses a bead system, which is pH released in the G.I. tract. 30% of the medication is delivered immediately, with the remaining 70% delivered over the next eight hours.

Ritalin LA is another bead system release for methylphenidate. It delivers half of the dose initially and the other half of the medication immediately, and then the other half 3 1/2 to four hours later.

Ritalin SR is a long-acting form of methylphenidate uses a wax matrix to provide the extension of its release. Many people taking this medication find that the medication releases inconsistently. This particular form is not commonly used.

Focalin XR A common practice among pharmaceutical manufacturers is to try to synthesize the mirror image of a molecule. These are called isomers. The properties of an isomeric form may be to reduce side effect profile, and often increase the potency per milligram of the medication. Focalin is the isomeric molecule for methylphenidate. In the extended release form, it will last between eight and 10 hours.

Most medications have better tolerability when taken with food. If a person has appetite suppression as a result of their medication, I will often advise people have a robust meal as they take their medication. With the medications that have a release activated by pH changes, citric acid in juices such as orange, grapefruit, and lemon juice and in Vitamin C can decrease the effectiveness of the medication. These should not be consumed at least one hour using your stimulant medication. Excretion of particularly amphetamines can be increased by the acidification of the urine. If a person is in the habit of drinking large amounts of citrus juice, this can potentially reduce the duration of response of stimulant medications.

Medication Interactions

Generally most medications are going to be fairly compatible with the use of psychostimulants. A class of medications called sympathomimetics, which include many cold remedies, particularly those containing pseudoephedrine, can increase the action of both medications. Antihistamines on the other hand, may diminish stimulants effectiveness. The best rule of thumb is to consult with a person who has prescribed to medications or a registered pharmacist. The latter will often have access to a variety of computer programs that elaborate interactions between medications. A pharmacist can be a wonderful source of information.

Non-stimulant Medications in the Treatment of Adult ADD

Strattera (atomoxetine). The precise mechanism of action for Strattera is not precisely known. It is believed to be selective inhibition of the pre-synaptic norepinephrine transporter. There is thought to be a secondary dopamine effect in the prefrontal cortex.

Strattera was the first medication marketed as a non-stimulant treatment for ADD/ADHD. It held a lot of promise for parents who did not wish to treat their children with stimulants, or for people with substance abuse disorders, where there was a concern for the stability of their sobriety. Many clinicians are quite hesitant to treat people with a history of substance abuse disorders for their ADD/ADHD. Strattera offered an alternative to stimulants. The advantage of this medication is that in a single daily dose, a person would have improvement in focus during all of their waking hours. When we refer back to the graph in figure 1, will note the small section noted as ATX. A relatively few number of people will have a differentially best response to this medication.

The side effect profile of this medication is the leading cause of discontinuation of the medication. Strattera can result in severe constipation, sexual side effects (to include retrograde ejaculation in males), dry mouth, nausea and weight gain. There is now a warning on this medication for use in children and adolescents for the potential for development of suicidal thoughts. The manufacturer advises close monitoring of this subpopulation.

There is also a possibility, albeit rare, of injury to the liver. Most prudent clinicians will monitor liver function tests at three months, and then every six months. This involves going to a laboratory for a blood test. This medication has to be used cautiously with people with cardiovascular disease, high or low blood pressure or rapid heart rate. There is also a risk for people with bipolarity spectrum disorders for this medication to push them into a manic episode. While this medication has its proponents, stimulants remain the first line, and most efficacious choice of medications for treatment of ADD/ADHD.

Many medications are used in what is called an "off label" application. This information gets passed along in a variety of ways to clinicians. The reason it doesn't get to the formal information that pharmacists have access to be financially driven. For a medication to be FDA approved for a particular use, it will involve extensive clinical trials and expense. Pharmaceutical companies operate out of the cost-benefit basis. If the medication has come off license and a generic formulation becomes available, there is very little financial benefit in having it approved for additional uses. Many of the non-stimulant medications employed for treatment of ADD /ADHD are "off label" uses of that medication.

SSRI's

There are a variety of classes of antidepressants that find their use into treatment of ADD/ ADHD. They may start with treating co-morbidities such as depression or anxiety disorders. The most common class for this treatment are SSRIs. Each has their own nuance of response. I like to use what I call the chocolate chip cookie analogy. There are many types of chocolate chip cookies. There are crunchy ones, soft ones, ones with dark chocolate, ones with milk chocolate or white chocolate. While they are all chocolate chip cookies, they are all different. Some SSRI's may be inherently more sedating or activating than others. A few are noted for a rapid washout of antidepressant response. It is not uncommon, particularly if a person has difficulties with anxiety for an SSRI to be paired with the psychostimulant.

By and large, these medications are well-tolerated. All medications have side effects. We think of things such as aspirin, as benign. They are common and millions and millions are taken every day without problem. If we were to read the side effect profile for aspirin, most of us would be quite wary about taking it. Most medications, across classes of medications, will have the nausea, vomiting, and diarrhea triad of symptoms. This is true for SSRI's is well. Some of the most difficult side effects are sexual in nature. For men, these side effects can delay ejaculation. For women, they can reduce drive and be a barrier to having an orgasm. Fortunately most people will not have the side effects. Serotonin containing medications are the first tier choice for treatment of all of the anxiety disorders. Anxiety is a very common comorbidity with ADD/ADHD.

Bupropion (generic form) is marketed under the trade name Wellbutrin®. It is also marketed under the trade name Zyban®, when it is employed for smoking cessation. It is exactly the same medication. This is an atypical stimulant-like antidepressant. There have been reports that it has some benefits in treating ADD/ADHD. While there is not a 100% correspondence in receptor sites, this antidepressant will affect norepinephrine and dopamine activity.

This is a fairly activating antidepressant. This can also lead to sleep disturbance, or increased anxiety. Fortunately there is now an extended release preparation. This preparation is far less likely to impair sleep. It is taken once a day, in the morning. The medication in the XL preparation is generic at 300 mg, and not generic at 150 mg. Due to the delivery system the tablet cannot be divided in half. Bupropion requires a stepwise titration to the target dose. Too rapid an increase in dose can reduce seizure threshold. This medication is generally not used for people with seizure disorders. One side effect is that of what is called "vivid dreaming." One client of mine described a dream of his that went from his normal black and white twofold color and surround sound. There was a car in a stream, and he recounted recalling what the tread on the tires looked like. Most people find this a pleasant experience, and are a little bit disappointed if it drops out of the side effect profile. This is a medication that should be carefully employed for people with night frights, and dreams related to PTSD. The last thing one wants to do is make difficult dreams even more vivid.

This antidepressant also has the potential to increase blood pressure. The people who are most at risk for this, are people who already have hypertension. When prescribing this medication, is prudent to measure your blood pressure 2-3 times per week. This doesn't mean you have to go out and purchase a blood pressure cuff, or keep going to fire stations for blood pressure checks. Many grocery stores and retail pharmacies have machines which will automatically take your blood pressure and pulse at the push of a button.

Bupropion is also considered the "go-to" medication if a person is experiencing sexual side effects from use of serotonin-based antidepressants. While it was commonly thought to be a poor choice for people with anxiety disorders, there is an assortment of literature that suggests benefit with anxiety disorders at therapeutic doses.

Tricyclic Antidepressants.

Tricyclic antidepressants (TCAs) were considered an alternative to stimulants in use with the pediatric population. They have advantages in terms of treating both anxiety and depression. For adults, most people required higher dosing to achieve a response in ADD/ADHD symptoms.

TCAs have had many drawbacks in terms of their use, and really are not commonly used at this point in time. Due to sedation, and the risk of lowering blood pressure, particularly when someone stands up, the dose needs to be increased very slowly. Many people cannot contend with the side effect profile. For these medications., this can include weight gain, blurred vision, constipation, dry mouth and sexual dysfunction. These medications also can elevate blood pressure and heart rate, and reduce cardiac conduction. The blood levels (serum levels) for TCAs are often quite variable. These are generally more risky medications in terms of CNS and cardiovascular toxicity.

Antihypertensives

Clonidine and Guanfacine are the two main medications that are used in the treatment of ADD/ADHD. They were first employed with children who had severe hyperactive or aggressive symptoms connected with their ADD/ADHD. The difficulty in use of these medications is they can be both sedative in nature, and cause a drop in blood pressure. The literature on this class of medications in the treatment of ADD/ADHD is far from extensive. They are not common medications found in most individual's treatment regime.

Medications are a tool. They are seldom the whole answer to addressing ADD/ADHD. Many people get quite a remarkable response, and do not find the need to seek intervention other than the use of medications. I encourage people to explore the variety of options that exist for coping with ADD/ADHD.

People will be best served by the use of a medication that has an extended release, and greater duration of hours of response. Short-acting medications have a very limited place in the arsenal of tools for clinicians. The drawback is having to take them multiple times per day, and often of rebound effect that leaves the person more unfocused than what they experience a baseline. Short-acting medications have the highest potential for abuse. Long-acting medications have relatively little value as a drug of abuse.

When creating a medication regime with methamphetamine salts or methylphenidate's, we want to find the dose which creates the best possible response. This involves a titration, or stepwise increasing in dose. The first dose is intentionally sub- therapeutic. The goal is to assess toleration. Side effects are likely to be less intense with a lower dosage. This stepwise increase in the amount of medication will progress with the goal of finding the point where more medication does not result in a better response. The individual then drops back a step. The other marker for dosage is the onset of new side effects. During the course of the titration, I have the person evaluate the response on a daily basis. The tool I have devised for this purpose will appear in the appendix. Your prescribing clinician is welcome to download this from: http://www.stimulusdrivenbrain.com. This tool prompts the person to think about the nuance of response. There is also a category called "effect on relationships." I like the person being treated to have their significant other provide additional input on this category. This often leads to a lively discussion between couples, in their varied forms, about the before and after effects on how they relate to one another.

If we regard relationships, and families like a mobile, if we change the size and shape of any one part, the whole system has to readjust. This is particularly true when a relationship has been a long-term one. Relationships develop equilibrium. Behavioral patterns develop that support that equilibrium. The given in life is that everyone copes in the best way that they know how. It may not be a way of coping that serves either the individual or the system well. Let's take the hypothetical example of a mother, living with an ADD adolescent. The teen comes into a room leaving a trail of book bags, shoes and coats. Mom feels antsy with clutter. It's a kinesthetic response that leaves her bordering on anxiety. She asks (and asks each time this behavior repeats), for change. "Could you please just take your things to your room and not leave things lying about?" The eyes roll. Perhaps the response is sullen because in the teen's head, this behavior is just not that big of a deal. The pattern continues until Mom finds it easier to just pick up behind their child rather than go through the same unchanging dance that she and her child do. Does Mom feel resentful or perhaps angry? You bet. She copes this way because she feels less angry than having to go through the same process time after time, with the same result. You can be the judge of whether this is ultimately a good way to cope.

Ken's Story

Ken was a 64-year-old man who had been married to his wife Betsy for 34 years. He had run a fairly successful environmental services consulting company. He served as adjunct faculty at a local business college, teaching two courses per year. He sought treatment because of his chronic disorganization, and his difficulty completing grading and evaluations for his college students. Before he started treatment, he questioned the use of treating ADD/ADHD given the fact he had planned to work one more year before retiring. His wife was eagerly looking forward to his retirement, and anticipated that they would now have the time to travel more.

Ken had a marvelous response to medications. He had remarked that he was more productive now than he had been at any time in his career. He was now questioning his decision to retire. His work in consulting and teaching had become in his words, "fun again." What had become clear is that during the course of his relationship, he had relied on Betsy to keep track of things for him. Suddenly he was able to do this for himself. This didn't stop Betsy from maintaining the role she had in their relationship for over 30 years. Ironically her efforts had become a source of irritation. Betsy had felt angry with his talk of continuing to work. The life she had looked forward to for a number of years seemed to be evaporating with Ken's new found enjoyment of his career.

Ken and Betsy followed my suggestion and entered into a brief course of couples counseling. They arrived at a reasonable compromise that they both could live with. He would work another 18 months at the level of his presence employment. This gave them a financial advantage in their retirement. At the end of that period of time, he would make a decision to either keep only his teaching, or only 50% of his consulting work. He had the advantage of having a partner in his business that could easily continue consulting business. This would allow him time to consider just what it was he loved doing most. During the course of therapy, Betsy had remarked to Ken's seeming a lot more "present" when they spend time together. Overall she found this something she enjoyed. Generally she found Ken tended to be less short tempered. Although this was difficult, she made very good strides in allowing Ken to do things for himself, rather than her jumping in and making sure things got done. From my perspective as a therapist, I believe in the use of self-reward when one pushes out the growing edges of one's life and coping. As a reward to themselves for making some fundamental changes in their relationship, Ken and Betsy decided to plan a trip to Paris.

Medications are a tremendous blessing for many people. They have had the horses to run with, so to speak. Medications can put all of those horses in the same harness and allow the person to direct their life in ways that were previously a struggle. They are a wonderful tool. If you have only one tool, say a hammer, then pretty quickly everything starts looking like a nail. Medication providers can sometimes fall into this unfortunate trap. Medications do not build skills. They do not teach a person how to organize or how to relate to the people they care about most in their lives. Both counseling and coaching can facilitate change in how one manages their life and how a person relates to others. They have an important place in really 'treating ADD/ADHD. Learning all that you can is important as well. I encourage my clients to become as well informed about all aspects of treatment. Here are some books I find useful in understanding and changing relationships if you or someone close to you has ADD/ADHD.

Book Suggestions:

1. A.D.D. & Romance by Jonathan Halverstadt

2. Is It You, Me, or Adult A.D.D.? Stopping the Roller Coaster When Someone You Love Has Attention Deficit Disorder By Gina Pera

3. You Mean I'm Not Lazy, Stupid or Crazy?!: The Classic Self-Help Book for Adults with Attention Deficit Disorder By Kate Kelly and Peggy Ramundo

·5·

The Adjustment to College

Any transition serious enough to alter your
definition of self will require not just small
adjustments in your way of living and thinking but
full on metamorphosis.
-Martha Beck

Change is the constant, the signal for rebirth, the
egg of the phoenix.
-Christina Baldwin

College can be more of a transition for the ADD/ADHD student. The student's parents may have provided more structure in assisting with meeting academic deadlines. High school may have added to this structure. Now daily routines will have to be established independently. There is the push-pull between competing social and academic demands. College may be where ADD/ADHD first becomes recognized. Many of my clients report that they slid through high school doing everything at the last minute. The workload was more manageable in high school. They didn't have the rapid fire of multiple assignments due in a smaller interval of time so they could put in a high degree of effort and get the job done.

The Younger Student and the Challenge of Social Relationships

The day has arrived that you've planned for since you were a junior in high school. Perhaps you have put college off for a while and only realized now is the time. You've arrived at college. With that comes the double edged sword of increased responsibility and increased freedom. You might've scoped out your roommate on Facebook, but now it's time to meet that person in the flesh. There's the chore of moving in, and figuring out how to make the shared space your own. The freshman orientation is right around the corner. You have your doubts about going.

Turn the clock forward by one month. The blush has left the apple, and the newness of the experience has worn off. There are times where you feel lonely. While family and friends are just a phone call away, it's just not the same. You ask yourself, 'Will I ever develop friends here?' No one else seems to admit to being homesick, but that fits what you feel is much as any other way of describing it. Your roommate has changed from the pretty cool person to an irritating, pain in the neck.

The first few weeks at college can often be quite a lonely time. The advantage of leaving the previously developed, set in stone, cliques that formed in high school, has turned out to be a catch-22. While going to college means swimming in a bigger pond, and a chance to reestablish oneself, without the baggage of your past life in high school, it is still a challenge. It is something every freshman faces.

The starting point is to first allow yourself enough time. You've probably come to the realization that your roommate is not automatically your best friend, or may not feel like a friend at all. Roommates are not set in stone. The first key to making new friends is to be who you are. In the larger social environment of college, everyone can find a group of people to form a support network. Realize also, that your old friends were not developed overnight. Be persistent. Get yourself out there and involved. A college or university environment, abounds with opportunities to meet people. The first place is the freshman orientation. By all means, go to it. As much as you might try and hide the fact that you are freshman, you're one of lots of other freshman. Every upperclassman was in the same position that you're in right now.

Class provides another opportunity to meet people. Form a study group. Connect with people who have the same course responsibilities, and automatically common ground to focus on. If you live in a dorm, generally there will be social events both formal and informal, and those can be take advantage of. Fraternities and sororities are yet another avenue to form a social group.

Go where your interest lies. Colleges have many opportunities for intramural sports. Religious groups have campus presence. First and foremost, college should not be just about going to class. Take advantage of volunteer activities. This may be both the most satisfying part of your college experience, and will be the tangible indicator of someone who has sampled deeply from the banquet table of what higher education has to offer. It is an opportunity to be broadened by the experience.

Roommates can often present special, often intense challenges and problems. There is the natural process of living with someone, and having to form boundaries which is a part of showing respect. Questions about sleep time, when to study, what to do about your roommate's visitors are a small sampling of the issues that face new roommates in what is often a very confined space. For everyone involved in higher education, the bar is raised in terms of workload. You and you alone need to take responsibility for why you're there. This often can mean negotiating, and directly asking for what you need. That discussion needs to be entered into commonly. It is a time to not label behavior, but describe it. There are two words, and two words only that make a request absolutely direct. These are, "Will You." This is not "can you," "would you," "I'd like you to," or an assortment of other ways of asking for your needs that are not absolutely direct. It has a 'yes or no' answer. If a roommate counters with, "I'll think about it", it is time to re-states that direct question. Either way, the answer gives you information. It states which your roommate will do, or will not do. At that point, it's time to decide what it is you need.

Forming a peer support group is essential to flourishing in college both socially and academically. People with ADD/ADHD may have the knowledge to form strategies but following carrying out those strategies is often a different matter. Negative attitudes may be a barrier to seeking help. This may be viewed as a sign of weakness or failure. The student may have had have always been an independent learner. Employing a group may be very different from what they have done to accomplish the tasks of school before. One way of addressing these concerns beyond study groups is to form a peer coaching group. It adds a degree of accountability to getting the tasks of school accomplished. It can be a means of getting non-judgmental encouragement in shifting how you accomplish the work of school. Student Services can be helpful in getting the word out that you want to form a peer coaching group.

Suggested Reading   http://www.thenakedroomate.com

This is the website for a very entertaining book. It has a great deal of very useful information about the transition to college. The book, The Naked Roommate and 107 Other Issues You Might Run Into in College is required reading at a number of colleges and universities. It is full of useful, practical advice on topics ranging from scholarships, sex, dating, relationships, video games, alcohol and drugs.

The Older Student

You might be called a non-traditional student. You look around you and you're the only one with a touch of gray hair. You feel like you've been driving longer than most of these kids have been alive. School for you may just be a means to an end. You've been confronted with the reality that moving ahead financially and in your career, and you need to add some letters behind your name. Maybe your previous academic life was a torturous and rocky road. If you are diagnosed with ADD/ADHD well into your adult years, you may be overcoming all beliefs about your capability. It may be that you're taking just one class, easing to your toe in the waters of academia.

Your reality is that when you finish a day at school, you will go home to other responsibilities. You may be a single parent, and have to deal with the needs of your children to eat, do their own homework and then bring order and organization to their lives as well as your own. Perhaps you have a spouse or significant other. While they are supportive, there are times you wonder if they feel like they're being ignored.

Life for the person who's balancing school and responsibilities that were in place before they started this process tends to become socially smaller. It will seem like there are fewer hours a day. It's easy to feel like any semblance of a social life gets crammed into the brief interval between quarters or semesters. Friends may wonder why you don't call. Before you start school, let them know that your free time will be drying up as a result of taking on this new challenge. Have a call and connect list that you address on weekends, just to let people know that you are still out there.

Sustaining relationships with your children can be a juggling act all by itself. Children need their time. They need frequency more than duration. When you are able to provide your children contact time, it is important that you are fully present. Do not split or tasks between being with them, and reading a book.

I made several rules for myself when I was in school. During my last trip to graduate school, I tried to make the point that we would have dinner as a family. The television would be turned off. There was no multi-tasking by bringing homework to the table. This was meant to be contact time where I could ask my son (and wife) about his (and her) day. Bedtime is also an opportunity for connection. On most nights we would take a few moments to just talk before he went to sleep. The foundation was laid for future behavior in our relationship. As I was starting my practice, I made a rule for myself that I would be done by 5 PM. My goal was to be able to be home for dinner for as long as he was still living in our house. The thread continues in that most Sunday evenings, we will have dinner together.

The role of the successful families is to accomplish two goals. The family allows the individual to first and foremost belong. The second goal is to allow its members to leave, and emancipate into their own separate life as an individual. The sense of belonging continues to be there even after they have established themselves in the world. If the investment in connection is not sustained, particularly during adolescence, the child will find other sources to meet those emotional needs. One of the dynamics in the formation of gangs is that the members are seeking connection. A commonality is lacking parental role models who are physically and psychologically present. Needs remain, even if unmet, as does the drive to fulfill them.

The needs of your spouse or significant other remain as well. As an adult, you're generally better at delaying gratification, and can sacrifice meeting your own meets to meet those of others. The divorce rate for couples with one partner in school is much higher than what we find in the general population. For most people who have been through college, relationships ending are very apparent. Most people don't think about the fact that the odds of your relationship continuing are heavily stacked against you when you enter college. You will be less physically and psychologically available. If you understand this, then you can avoid some of the pitfalls.

Decide early in the process to set aside quality time or your spouse or significant other. The cost of going to school is often a lack of spontaneity within a relationship. Quality time tends to be more structured and planned. The benefit of arranging to have a date, or a plan to have sex is that these things will happen. It is all too easy to get caught up in the process, and the things that sustain and enhance the quality of a relationship fall by the wayside. Often a few sessions with a professional counselor can be of enormous help in making some beneficial changes in relationship. Realistically you will probably need to make a few course corrections in the manner in which you support each other.

The story of one partner sacrificing their growth and development so the other partner can go to school is an old one, too often repeated. It is one partner experiencing the people and events, he/she can grow distant from his/her partner.. If the split occurs in a relationship, the other partner rightfully can feel used. The supporting partner may stop embracing his/her own graph, stagnation can occur.

It is important for the partner who is not in school to realize that continued growth as a couple involves the growth of not one partner but both. Your partner doesn't dream your dreams. Inasmuch as they might share those aspirations they must also move in any direction that is uniquely fulfilling for them. School may not be where their dreams lie. Where are the growing edges of their life? How do they stimulate and fulfill themselves independent of the relationship? It is not surprising that the odds of the relationship enduring are better if both partners are in school. There is an appreciation for the demands that each person faces. Both people are in the process of rapid growth. A perspective that "we are in this together", often brings a couple closer. If your spouse or significant other cannot answer these questions, then these are signposts marking danger on the relationship road. Again a few sessions with a skilled counselor can be well worth the investment. Consider doing this before you start the process. Once you are in the whirl wind of high demand, it will be harder to find the time. Taking a thought from the field of medicine, prophylaxis is far less expensive than treating illness. Affordability? How much does divorce cost? Remember, the odds of your relationship surviving are heavily stacked against you. Have your relationship be in the minority of those which survive.

Depression

Depression is frequently a feature found with ADD. Some studies show the incidence as high as 39% for individuals age 14-18 (1). There are studies that show there is a family link between depression and ADD/ADHD (2). The presence of ADD/ADHD and a concurrent bipolarity spectrum disorder is often difficult to separate. Many of the symptoms of ADD/ADHD mirror those found with bipolar disorder (3). For the person with ADD, depression is a more frequent occurrence.

Depression is something that will affect one person in every five during the course of their life. It may affect us, or our roommate or friends. That means, if you know 100 people, 20 of them will experience a depression severe enough that it requires some level of intervention. The only advantage to depression in how common it is, is the fact that it is quite treatable. It is only treatable, if a person gets help.

So how do we recognize depression, as opposed to sadness or loneliness, both in our self or in others? Depression has a physical component. For the most part, people will lose energy. It will be hard for a person to get started in the morning. Getting out of bed can be a real chore. Greatly increased or decreased, sleeping is frequently a marker for a shift in mood. Becoming more socially withdrawn, or disconnected from others can be a hallmark feature.

How do I bring it up with my roommate, or friend, if I see this process going on for them? The answer is -directly! Realize that depression has a mortality rate. It also has a big cost in terms of the satisfaction and joy one can experience in their life. First and foremost, it is treatable. Pass the person directly if they're having feelings that life isn't just worth living, or if they're having thoughts of hurting himself in some way. To quote a timeworn expression, "you can lead a horse to water, you can't make him drink," and the same goes in the case of depression. However, you should strongly encourage a person to get some help.

All colleges and universities have some provision for their students to obtain this type of help. If it is a very small school, they will have someone in student services that has a referral list of people that students can go talk to. Many medium to larger size schools have counseling programs. If a school contains a medical school or a Masters or doctoral program, often there is an affiliated clinic, where senior residents, and degreed candidates can provide counseling support, and referral to community resources.

If you're experiencing depression, it is a life lesson to realize that you alone are responsible for caring for your needs. Help us out there. If you have someone you know, and it seems to you that they're having a struggle with depression, say something. Offer your support by getting them pointed in the right direction. This doesn't mean that you have to take on the responsibility of being their therapist. You can share your empathy. You can point them in the right direction, and most of all, encourage them to get help.

Resources

http://www.campusbluew.com
This is a great website that provides a lot of information about depression, and finding resources.

http://www.psycheducation.org
This is a rich and reliable source of information about depression, bipolarity and ADD/ADHD. It contains numerous mental health topics.

·6·

The Study Environment

It is singularly ironic that we devote far more effort
to develop optimal habitat for zoo animals than we
do for our own species.
-*Heerwagen et al. (1995)*

Take a trip to a modern day zoo. The exhibit will try to recreate the natural environment where the animal is found. We no longer look through chain-link fence, sheets of Plexiglas or barred cages. The enclosure incorporates this task without them being visually apparent. Animals are no longer kept in concrete cubicles, which are small, uncomfortable, and have little thoughts for their physical or emotional years.

In recent years, more consideration and attention has been given to the housing of animals in zoos than the work environment for people. The zoo that does not pay attention to the animal psychological needs in creating a comfortable environment receives a great deal of pressure from the community to step up to the current standard for care.

Unfortunately, the same cannot be said for many public buildings particularly the public study spaces for students. These can be some of the worst environments for the ADD college student. Even in this day and age little thought is given to the psychological needs of the people who will use the spaces. The workspaces available to students are little removed from the cubicle land described in Dilbert. Worse yet are open areas of tables, with no separation from fellow students, and at times having the appearance of an educational sweatshop.

The same lack of concern and creativity can be found in the workplace, where the impact of environment. This disregard for the comfort it needs of people who actually use a building stems from the belief that people can easily adapt to their environment. Design focuses primarily on function, providing the bare necessities to perform a task, while keeping the building and maintenance costs at a minimum. In both academia and in the workplace, standardized structures are the norm, with little consideration given to individual differences.

Over the last couple of decades, a new discipline has evolved which explores the impact of environment on an individual's disposition, development, and production. Environmental psychologists have studied people in a wide variety of work, study, and living environments just to see how much they are affected by their surroundings. Predictably, they found that most people seek and prefer environments that are most compatible with the needs and preferences, a condition they term "person-environmental congruence." Taking their findings a step further, they also discovered that, when the environment is not compatible, nor can be modified to become compatible with an individual's needs, feelings of stress, dissatisfaction, and dissention often result.

This is a particularly acute difficulty for the person with ADD/ADHD. When physical and psychological comfort is absent, it is not unusual for the mind to be more distracted. One symptom that is not uncommon for people with ADD/ADHD is to be very sensitive to both noise and to touch. In a less than optimum or negative study environment, attention needs to be made to control of the environment and the student's physical comfort.

The Negative Environment

An environment can evoke a negative response to its inhabitants in a variety of ways. Poor environmental conditions, including light, air quality, temperature, noise, crowding, lack of privacy, and the inability to control social interaction are just a few. Let's take a look at the typical college library, as excellent example of the negative environment.

1. **Poor lighting.** Fluorescent lighting, the most common kind used, serves a functional need for a large number of people, but does little for the individual. It creates a high-glare work environment. Many people find themselves

sensitive to the high-frequency oscillation that fluorescent lights off and half.

2. **Too hot/too cold.** Many libraries have large open spaces with high ceilings, making temperature regulation difficult.

3. **Too many people.** Crowding is an inherent problem found in libraries. Even when not crammed with people, libraries have a constant flow of traffic, contributing to levels of distraction and noise.

4. **No privacy.** Library users have little control over social conditions. We now live in a cell phone culture, where people have an almost obsessional need to be connected throughout the course of their waking hours. While we can control our own distraction with our own cell phone, we are at the mercy of everyone else's use. Private spaces within the library are often difficult to access or are nonexistent.

5. **Too distracting.** The people making sure that the library works, checking books out, wheeling books through the stacks returning them to their proper place, add to the external stimulation found in libraries.

6. **Libraries are just too loud.** Noise contributes to a whole host of negative effects in the learning environment.

These include:

· Decreased cognitive abilities.
· Memory impairment.
· Cognitive fatigue.
· Decreased comprehension on complex tasks.
· Decreased task persistence.
· Stress response of increased physiological arousal.
· Decreased task satisfaction.

The Positive Environment

As an example of the positive environment, let's take a look at a typical home. Within a home, there are places where people seem to gather. While this may reflect the functional aspects of a room, people are naturally drawn to psychologically compatible spaces. When "person-environmental congruence," as the environmental psychologists call it, occurs, people experience positive feelings which lead to positive outcomes. How many times at social gatherings had people all crowded into the kitchen. The smell of cooking food will draw people in. People may have other space available to them but are draw to the space with the highest degree of psychological and social comfort. The psychological compatibilities influenced by an individual's perception of an environment is pleasant and inviting. Natural light, particularly some light, and a view to the outdoors, create a positive perception of spaciousness and decrease in negative perception of being closed in.

Researchers have found that workers in a windowless space suffer for more negative feelings about their work than their counterparts with access to exterior light and a view of outside space. A windowless space also affects people's sense of relative time and may throw off their circadian rhythms, because they are given no visual clues as to whether it is day or night. One environment where I currently work is the psychiatric portion of the emergency room. It is a windowless box. In the course of my 12 hour shift, but I may never see the outside light during the course of the day. During the wintertime, I come and leave in the dark. After my third day in a row, my internal sense of time becomes badly skewed. The unfortunate part of this work environment is that it is intensely fluorescent, and does not use full spectrum balls. Lighting can create variability of light and shadow. Often the color of the walls can add to the psychological warmth of an environment. In the ideal, steering away from paint finishes which have high-gloss will reduce the glare factor. Decorating with plants can enhance a sense of spaciousness.

In the design of the study space, person-environmental congruence entails both functional and psychosocial components.

This they should be neither too large nor too small, and include a desktop large enough to open books and notebooks simultaneously, and be equipped with readily accessible resources. When possible, books, computer access, and phone should be kept within easy reach of the workspace. Keep everything within easy reach to lessen the chance of becoming distracted and losing focus during the study time.

The goal is to be able to stay at one's desk for a fairly extended period of time. The space needs to be comfortable enough to avoid getting up and walking to other parts of one's living space. This opens the door to becoming distracted. One will see many things that need doing, but the reality is, making sure plant has water, or the mail is brought inside will only distract you from getting work done.

Physical comfort is important considering the number of hours spent in the workspace. Libraries typically take a "one-size-fits-all" approach to seating. The chair that fits a person who is 5 feet tall doesn't work well for a person who is over 6 feet tall. For the private study space, investing in a comfortable chair that suits the individual is a wise expenditure. Having a desk that fits both person and share is also a must.

What is the ambience or atmosphere of the room? Is the room of visually pleasant place to spend time in. Ambience supports both functional and psychosocial congruence. Factors such as comfort, low glare lighting, reduced visual clutter, variation colors and textures in a row, and use of the verse objects to increase the spatial interest in a row all contribute to psychological comfort.

Does the workspace allow its resident to control both privacy and social interaction? The door is one of the truly underrated developments in human social history. Close the doors to the outside world. Turn the ringer off your phone, and let voicemail do its work.

Psychological compatibilities further accomplished by personalizing the study environment. Our territory is often defined by her belongings, as there is comfort in just being around our "stuff." When older adults move to smaller housing, one of the most difficult aspects is parting with their belongings, in effect giving up their unique identity. We decorate our homes in ways that make them pleasant to us. Memories live within objects in space. Personalizing a new space with our belongings gives us a concrete connection is passed positive associations and increases are psychological comfort. A new place, in say a dormitory, seems far less foreign and more like it belongs to us if we personalize our space.

Tips for Creating and Improving Study Space

· Arrange furniture so that phone, computer, and books are within easy reach of one another.

· Put up a bulletin board close to the study area to easily post needed school-related reminders.

· Choose a study space with a window.

· Cover crowded bookcases with inexpensive fabric to create a visual barrier, and give the appearance of neatness by reducing visual clutter.

· Invest in spotlight-type lamps or upwardly directed floor labs to bounce light off the ceiling and reduce glare. Can lighting, placed on the floor and surrounded by plants, creates light and shadow for more visual interest in a room.

· Create a large, inexpensive desk with a hollow core door and a couple of file cabinets. For more finished look, attach molding to the edges and apply some stain. Fabric that can be used to apply more unconventional colors that still allow the wood to show through. Make a surface water and stain resistant with spray polyurethane. Having a large workspace allows the student to have everything within easy reach. This is particularly useful when it comes to applying the skills explained later in the book for writing papers.

· Bring plants into the environment to make the room seem more alive. Many colleges and universities have greenhouses where students are permitted to take cuttings of unusual plants at no cost.

- Have on hand a small fan, which circulates the air and provides white noise to mass background sounds. A portable space heater can accommodate different comfort levels for temperature when sharing a study space.

- Hunt for mismatch sheets at department stores. They are often less expensive than slip covers for beat up stuffed chairs and couches. A comfortable chair can provide a relaxing alternative from a desk chairwhen a person has a lot of reading.

- Make or buy a "Do Not Disturbed" sign for the outside of your room. If you share housing, negotiate with the house rules should be regarding sound and interruptions during times were you need to study.

·7·
Maximizing Our Potential to Learn

Researchers have shown that some regions of the
adult brain stay as malleable as a baby's brain,
so we can grow new connections, strengthen
existing connections and even create new neurons,
allowing us all be life- long learners.
-John Medina from Brain Rules (2008)

Our entry into the sensory experience of the world literally bombards us with information. Our task at birth is to make sense of that sensory world. As infants, we gradually connected that our hands and our arms are part of our physical self. As vision clears, we learn certain faces will nurture us in a variety of ways that are essential to our survival. Bodily contact becomes associated with the visual clue of the faces of our parents and caregivers. Over time, the sounds and voices take on meaning and an association is made between the visual and auditory world. Words still do not have meaning, but the tone, cadence and the voices of our parents and caregivers do. Soon voices become recognizable even in the absence of visual cues, and a touch or a word can comfort in infants distress, even in the absence of visual cues.

The maturing brain progressively becomes more adept at learning to process information received by sound, touch, and vision. We learn to perceive our world through our senses. As we develop, we begin to identify form and function. Perceptual learning takes place in the sensory association cortex, with each sense accorded its own. The infant develops circuits of neurons, which recognize the complex stimuli within the environment, and learning is presumed to be accomplished by changes in synaptic connections.

In the late 1970s, Richard Bandler and John Grinder developed the communication theory, which they'd named neuro-linguistic programming (NLP). Their development of this theory was intended for application and psychotherapy, but it can also be useful in understanding learning style and developing more effective ways of learning.

Bandler and Grinder put forth the theory that our thinking occurs in three main representational systems: creating visual images, hearing sounds, and making sensory contact with the physical world. An individual will use all representational systems, but generally, one will become the dominant system used. All of the representational systems operate all of the time, but only part of this information enters consciousness.

Analyzing the creative process can help us understand the concept of representational systems. If you are not musically inclined, ask your friends who are how they can remember the notes to play for each piece of music without having the written notes in front of them. When they look at a piece of sheet music, how do they translate this into a melody by applying the notes on their instrument, or having a sense of the melody in their mind. Often these people will describe their experiences as hearing the sounds in their head.

Have you ever had difficulty deciphering a word when someone spells it aloud to you, and yet you immediately recognized the same word once you see it written? Or think about learning how to find an unfamiliar place. Do you prefer written directions, or is a map more helpful. Both of these examples reflect the different learning styles which are hardwired into our brains by the time we become adults. More kinesthetically inclined people learn better through tactile experience. Once they play with an object, they know how it works. We have all known children who get into trouble. They seem compelled to touch everything they see. As frustrating as this behavior is for their parents, it is more likely a representation of how that child learns, rather than a sign of disobedience. Touch is fundamental to their ability to process information about their environment, and key to their learning.

You may wonder whether you are oriented visually, auditory, or kinesthetically. The truth is, we employ all representational systems to some extent. No doubt you feel you know, which way you learn best. This knowledge can be both a help and a hindrance, for assuming that you learn best in one way may limit you from using other systems to support the primary learning method. The challenge, therefore, is to use your strongest process of learning as a pathway to efficiency, but remained open to using other techniques so that you can learn on as many levels as possible.

I experience the power of using multiple representational systems and helping my son learned to spell. Spelling presented unique difficulties for him as he had a learning disability that impacted sequencing and pattern recognition (ADD/ADHD). My son would spell words in a shallow pan of rice or a pan of shaving cream, saying the words out loud as he did so. This method used all three representational systems -visual, auditory, and kinesthetic, -simultaneously. Once we started using this method, his spelling tests showed remarkable improvement.

Anchoring is another concept from neuro-linguistic programming. My own son's learning ability is definitely at its best with a hands-on physical approach to learning. To help him recall the spelling of words, we developed 'spelling wrestling. To be released, he would have to spell a word correctly. If he didn't spell it correctly, and I would make a loud sound like a buzzer and tickle him. After a bit of encouragement to sound things out, he would spell the word correctly and be released. This would pair multiple representational system and anchor the spelling of words in his memory.

My son was always eager to tackle this wrestling approach to learning how to spell. Not only did it help him anchor the spelling words, it provided positive contact and a great deal of fun for us. What was once a struggle for him became an enjoyable time, and gave him the opportunity to succeed at the difficult task. Studying spelling words turned from tedium, and something that would always leave his stimulus driven brain to wander to something that made learning much more fun.

So what is anchoring? Think of Pavlov's famous experiment, where the dogs salivated at the sound of the ringing bell. We know this is a stimulus-response conditioning. Anchoring is similar in that it introduces another dimension of the sensory experience in to the active representational system a person uses, which serves as an "anchor" for the learning taking place. In my son's example, there was a physical, kinesthetic anchor for recalling the sequences of spelling words. The anchor was a powerful learning tool because the emotional pleasure of the activity, that of touching, laughing, and having fun with one of his parents.

We all have experiences in our lives which have been anchored by multiple sensory inputs, some of which are only cognitively experienced in one's system. How often have you heard a particular song that reminds you of a particular time and place in your life? You can remember exactly what you were doing, who you were with, and approximately where you were in your life. This is a frequent and fairly universal occurrence. These are anchored experiences. We can use this concept to increase the ability to absorb retained and recall information.

This is largely a temporal lobe functioning. It is in this part of the brain were sequencing skills are developed. It is also in part responsible for memory. It is not unusual for people with ADD/ADHD have difficulty recalling information. It is not like they don't know the information, but it's pulling it into the conscious mind to relate it. The more we can connect the recall of information to multiple representational systems, the easier information is to bring forth information forth from our memory.

Studying chemistry provides a good example of how anchoring can be used to learn. Many students find learning how chemical compounds react to be quite abstract and difficult to grasp. They are left to struggle with learning how to make sense of chemistry by rote learning of rules for combining elements. While rote learning can be useful, even necessary in many cases, learning improves when it moves from the abstract to the tangible.

Chemistry students who need help recalling abstract information can buy inexpensive model sets for building chemical models. As they put together these models, they simultaneously use multiple neurological circuits. What is two-dimensional in the textbook becomes three-dimensional in their hands. Now those neuron groups that deal with spatial relationships are brought into play, and this is kinesthetic is a learning element which anchors the information in yet another representational model.

Years from now, if you have access to your child's modular building set, you might find yourself making a perfect Benzene ring or other complex compound. That's when you'll truly know that you have anchored that piece of learning.

Efficiency: Learning in High Fact Volume Situations

As we have discussed, there are many methods for retaining information, all of which require some degree of repetition. By now, you probably have an idea which representational system you use best. The key is to find a combination of systems that will let you learn most efficiently.

Let's take an example of trying to retain information from a lecture. Most students take notes to accomplish this, although this approach can actually impede thinking about information as it is given. For the student with ADD/ADHD, use of the note taker can be quite useful in allowing one to not be distracted by splitting one's attention to take notes. Having someone to take notes is a commonly asked for accommodation, that is provided for in the Americans with Disabilities Act. It alleviates the student and having to fully focus on two tasks at the same time. Some students may take the lecture and then transcribe it from notes. This employs both auditory and kinesthetic representational systems, but can be fairly labor-intensive. A more efficient plan would be to make brief flash cards while listening to a taped lecture. Not only do you review the material by making the cards, you can then use the cards to repeatedly review the material.

This type of strategy is often used in successful marketing campaigns. Marketing theorists have developed what they call "the rule of sevens," which states that to retain a piece of information, the minimum number of repetitions needed is seven. Successful product owe much of their success to use of repetition of their advertising message rather than their intrinsic value.

The same theory can be applied to studying. When the number of repetitions of a piece of information is increased, the ability to recall the information is enhanced. Many fields of study have a high volume of facts students must be able to recall. Law and medicine are two examples. In a typical anatomy and physiology course, the student will need to memorize in excess of 400 facts in a typical week. Repetition is essential.

Flashcards are an excellent tool for achieving high fact volume learning. They're effective for those who learn best through visual system. Saying the information aloud will hope the person who has developed and auditory representational system. While creating each card, the auditory student can use the lecture tapes as repetition of the material.

For the person who has a kinesthetic representational system, there are many ways to physically anchor the information. The very act of writing the cards is a physical anchor. Reviewing the cards while performing some physical tasks, such as walking or riding a stationary bike, is another way to add a physical anchor to the visual stimuli reading the card. When a student has a tangible structure to remember, like the chemistry molecules mentioned above, reviewing the cards while handling the object is helpful. Having flashcards handy during lab time, is a great way to get the most out of the experience.

What makes an effective flash card? Just going down the information allows you to review the data, but you want to get more than that free investment of time. The design of cards should reflect your overall strategy for attacking the content of the course, which is usually based on how the instructor tests for information. In many types of courses, rote reproduction of information is neither how the instructor tests, nor the best way to retain information into long term memory. Integrating material and understanding relationships of allows you to transfer information to other related problems.

Let's take an example of integration from the field of law. Law students are required to recall the details of many cases. The sheer facts are not necessarily what is most important. Writing the implication of decisions on your flash card is a way of linking the importance of the information with the particulars of the case.

Seven Great Tips for Increasing the Effectiveness of Flash Cards

1. Pull not only the facts out of a piece of information, but why the information is important. How will the instructor asked you to integrate the information? Your card should address this.

2. But only information that you don't know on flashcards.

3. State the question on one side and the answer on the flip side. Phrase the question too closely reflect the style of the instructor. This question/answer format provides immediate feedback on correct answers, which reinforces learning.

4. Color-code the upper corner of a card to easily group cards littered topically related. Learning is enhanced when you review cards with similar topics and concepts.

5. Use highlighters to make key facts are heading standout. The use of color provides a subtly more complex stimulus, implying the individual bundles of neurons of the primary visual cortex, which recognize color. This broadens the type of neural circuits involved to recall information. You several colors markers to highlight information, using one color on all cards to relate to a particular concept or topic. Resist the temptation to highlight too much. Stick to the most important words or concepts.

6. Reproduced diagrams from handouts and textbooks using the copy machines reduction setting. Paste the diagrams on flashcards, using whiteout fluid to remove labels to parts of the diagram. A second copy can be pasted on the reverse side allowing a question and answer format with diagrams. Instructors usually use the same diagram on tests as they do on handouts.

7. Use mnemonics to help recall sequences and concepts. Mnemonics are an excellent way to key recall for difficult, or complex information.

Mnemonics

A mnemonic, simply defined, is a memory technique based on association. This type of memory training dates back to the early Greeks and Romans. A speaker associated parts of their discourse with parts of their homes. The opening of the speech would be associated with aspects of the opening to their homes. Successive ideas would then be associated with a mental journey of something very familiar, walking through their house. Simonides, who lived around 500 B.C., is regarded as the father of the arts of trained memory. He believe that memory training was important further development of the thinking process.

Our ability to remember relies heavily on association, and much of the association takes place on a subconscious level. For the learner, the task is to make conscious associations with new information that may be intangible or abstract. Recall becomes easier when information has some meaning in a person's world. After this new information is incorporated into memory and cognitively process, it takes on meaning and becomes easier to remember.

Music provides a good example of the use of mnemonics to assist learning. The lines on a music staff – E, G, B, D, and F, are totally abstract for the beginning student. Initially they have neither relevance nor meaning. Music teachers commonly used the sentence "Every Good Boy Does Fine," as a means of helping students recall the musical staff. While the sentence is not familiar, it is understandable. The understandable becomes linked with the abstract, taking the first step into incorporation of memory. Not only do the letters of the musical staff become easily remembered, the order or sequence of the musical staff becomes easily recalled.

In developing your own mnemonics sentences, the words in the sentence should follow the natural order or the sequence that the information has. Anatomy provides many examples of order. Take a spinal column, which has five divisions. They are, from the top to the bottom, the cervical, thoracic, lumbar, sacral, and coccyx. A mnemonic which views the learner to names and sequence of the divisions is "Country Texans Love Other Comfort." The visual learner may naturally form a visual picture of drunken cowboys sitting around sipping Southern Comfort. Forming a mental picture of the mnemonic and further enhances the recollection of the mnemonic for all learners.

When creating a mnemonic device, humor is an important asset. Risqué and humorous mnemonics are often recalled for many years. Try to be amusing and clever and coming up with a mnemonic. It adds an element of fun to the task of learning.

Many fields of study have published books of mnemonic devices. While it can be fun to venture own, sometimes there's a relief in having it already done for you. A book of some topic specific mnemonics is a good investment.

Chunking Information

Most people can only process five to nine pieces of information at once. More than that exceeds the person's ability to contain information. One way to learn more rapidly, and learn the most complex tasks is to chunk information into small steps. They then are reassembled into the original whole. Let's take a spelling example. The medical field is full of complex drug names. Let's take methylphenidate, one of the major classes of stimulant found in treatment of ADD/ADHD. We want to break it down into three smaller chunks of information. Take a piece of paper and write the three parts of the word on it, then hold them above and to the left of your eyes. See "methyl", and close your eyes and see it in your mind. Now open your eyes. Continue to do these five or six times until you can close your eyes and clearly see methyl. Next take the second chunk of information. See "pheni", and repeat the same steps with this chunk of information, picking up the pace. Now repeat this with "date". Do this until the entire image of methylphenidate is stored in your mind. Once you have a clear picture, you might notice that feeling of being sure you have now learned the word. This is a kinesthetic linking.

Once you have a clear picture, and can see the word broken down into three chunks, you will be able to spell it both forward and backward. Take a moment to give this a try. Spell methylphenidate. Spell it backwards. You are now going to be able to spell this word forever. You can apply this technique to learning, any word, in any field of study.

Speaking as a person who is a notoriously poor speller, and labeled as someone who is dyslexic, I needed to pay attention to my own learning style. Much of this was kinesthetic, followed by visual. Standard teaching is typically visual or auditory. The method of teaching was not well suited to my strongest way of learning. What I had was not a learning disability but   a disability in what strategy I would use. Chunking became a way to mastery by employing a bear a different strategy. This is the value of learning what your own learning strategy is.

·8·

The Paper Swamp: Conquering Clutter and Dismissing Disorganization

Efficiency is intelligent laziness.
-David Dunham

The more demand you have on your time, the greater your need for organization. Organization allows you to both keep track of all of those many demands each day places on you and efficiently address them. For all of us who are trying to cram as much as we can into a 24 hour day, organization is essential.

I have noticed that people often defined themselves as inherently organized or disorganized. Such an observation stems from a belief rather than an irreversible reality. A belief system can be changed, simply by experiencing success within a new belief system. The truth may be that you simply don't have the tools you need to become organized. This chapter is about getting the right tools and creating a new belief system. You can be an organized person!

A good place to start your reorganization is with an analysis of your environment. Look around. Does your study space suffer from excessive clutter? It's time to throw out the notion of organized chaos. Admit that you don't know where everything is in that mess. If you have stacks of paper, even if they are sorted, all you have are sorted stacks of paper. Even when you get around to shuffling through the stacks of paper, what's the point if you have no place to put them once they are organized!

You need a place to store things. Invest in a file cabinet and dividers (about $50 in most areas). Give some thought to other tools that you will need, such as a daily calendar on which you can write your agenda and an easy to use Rolodex. Buy everything you need in one shopping trip.

Once you have your equipment in place, you can put into practice the guiding principle for keeping your desk organized: the first time you touch a piece of paper is also the time you act on. This is another way of saying that you want to try to take care of things as they come up. For example, when I open mail, I plan on the time to resolve anything which presents as a task. This may sound unrealistic given the demands of the student, but it can be done. Take an action oriented approach to keeping clutter out of your workspace by the following.

Top 10 Tips to Organize Your Work Space

1. Set up a filing system that allows you to access information quickly and easily. Label files with short, generic names; don't be so specific or you'll end up with a lot of files, many with very little in them. Avoid giving in to the impulse to label one file "Miscellaneous," which translated means "disorganized collection of things you won't readily be able to find." Before you know it, it will have grown too fast with this similar information, defeating the purpose of a filing system.

2. "When in doubt, throw it out." This adage has been around for a long time, and it is just as true now as when the unknown efficiency expert created it. We've all heard the horror stories about mothers who throughout childhood collections of Barbie's and baseball cards are now selling for fortune on the Internet. Still, I suggest you take this saying to heart, because it offers some good advice. If you can't file an item and you can figure out some specific future need for it, best to get rid of it.

3. Use a day-timer or calendar to record meetings, appointments, and other time sensitive information. I've heard more than one person say, "My brains are in my calendar." Ironically, those are the people I considered to be smart, for they don't clutter their minds with trying to remember some appointment in the distant future. With a day-timer or pocket calendar, you have everything you need to organize your time, and keep it at your fingertips.

No more looking for scrap paper on which you hastily wrote down an appointment time. No more scheduling an appointment only to realize that you have a conflict. With the day timer, you have better control of your time, which saves you time. With advances in technology, our cell phone or similar device can now be that organizer. As we make the choice to be more connected, we can take advantage of readily available tools to help organize our life. We can literally do everything from checking our e-mail, to keeping our appointments and giving us an audio reminder of what we need to attend to, and store it all in our pocket.

4. Devise a system for paying bills in a timely manner. One way to do this is to file a bill in an accordion file as soon as you receive it. You will pay at the same time, usually twice pr month. Mark you pay date on your calendar. For those of you who want to stick with the "touch it only once practice, pay it when you open it. That way, you will never be delinquent on a payment, which can carry a stiff financial penalty.

5. Keep your library of information up to date. For example, if an acquaintance calls you with a new phone number, address, or e-mail address, make the immediate change to your Rolodex or your address book. I had the habit of keeping business cards and bits of paper with friends phone numbers stuffed in my wallet. It would take awhile to locate a number when I wanted it. My wallet eventually became too large to fit comfortably in my back pocket. If you have to take your wallet out of your back pocket to drive comfortably, it's time to purge. I haven't broken myself of this habit completely, but now I periodically clean the cards and scraps of paper and put them where I can readily access them. With business cards, I will either stapled them right into the Rolodex, or place them in a ring binders specifically designed to hold business cards. I also know the context in which I have acquired a card. For those I feel might not be self-evident. I can,

of course, recall who my friends are; the same may not be true for someone I meet at a party or a seminar. When someone calls whom I have met only briefly, I simply spin my Rolodex to their name and instantly recall who he or she is, take in the background information on the card, and jump right into the conversation. People are generally quite pleased that I've remember them, even though our previous contact was minimal.

When you organize all the information about the people you know, in one place, it not only save yourself time, you create a tremendous network which can be useful years into the future. Classmates, professors, advisors, friends, colleagues, mentors, coaches, teammates and professional peers, all of these people are worth having in your address book, Rolodex or a file on your computer. They may be valuable to you when you come to look for work in your field. You may want to store them in an Outlook file. Use of this tool allows you to contain far more information. It's only down side is that it may be far less portable.

6. Deal with incoming correspondence in one of two ways: Either take care of it or file it for future reference. Assign a time to respond to it. I find the best time to answer letters is after I finished with any school oriented work for the day. Writing to friends or family takes less effort than studying. And writing personal letters or e-mails provides a more satisfying end to the day.

7. Reduce your clutter by keeping books and magazines organized on the bookshelf when not actively in use. Periodicals provided by an instruction can be filed in the class notebook, and the notebook shelved as well. Put the class synopsis in a clear pocket that will go in front of a three ring notebook for a class. Keep a different binder for each course.

8. Get rid of magazines that are more than two months old. Consider donating them to a place where others will enjoy reading them. Nursing homes, the gym, the

library even local jails are just a few places they can use recent magazines. If the magazine contains something you want to retain, put the information in a computer file or file it away in the appropriate file. The standing rule I have in my office, is that if a client is reading a magazine more than one month old, they are welcome to take that magazine with them. This has solved the problem of dated magazines and excessive clutter. Catalogs should have n even shorter residence time. If you haven't ordered anything from them in two weeks, you're probably not going to. Dump them into the recycle bin.

9. The connected world of text messaging and receiving e-mail over our phone is a massive time vampire. It is an easy distraction for the ADD/ADHD person. How many times have we felt someone was not fully present because of the distraction of them checking a text message or an e-mail right when their phone alerts them to new messages. We may even be that person. I have given up checking my e-mail in the morning. It is the least effective time to do it. I tell my business colleagues and clients, I will check my e-mail twice per day, at about noon and at the end of the business day. Wait until the end of the study day to answer social calls and respond to e-mail. Use this as wind down time

10. Keep a neat, well organized desk, for this is a springboard to overall organization. Give some thought to how you want to set up your study place. For example, a rack above, or next to your desk where you can store items that you will want to have on hand for your studies. That day will help keep you focused on your assignment. By gathering everything you need in one, convenient spot, you won't constantly be interrupting your work get one more thing to complete your task.

Organize the Day

Planning your day is essential to keeping yourself organized in on track. I begin each day looking at my day timer. This provides you an initial review of what classes you have and when. Putting reminders in the day timer of major projects and when they are due helps make sure you don't forget to bring assignments to class. The same skills readily translate to the work world. I see which clients are coming in. Any testing I've completed with me at home gets included in my bag before I leave for the day. I see if I'm on call. This lets me know how much time margin I have for the end of the day. It's handy to the point where I know whether to take a lunch or if I'm going out during my mid-day break.

Making a list is the most efficient way to stay on track with a task oriented day. When you write down what you wish to accomplish during the day, you can better prioritize your list of things to do. You will also save yourself time by seeing what can be bunched together. An added benefit is that your memory is prompted to remember various tasks. How many of times have you gone to the grocery store knowing what you needed and returned home having forgotten something? Make a list!

Don't overlook that satisfying feeling that comes with crossing tasks off your list that you may have completed. When you can physically see what you have done during the day, your time and efforts become more tangible. You are left with a sense of real accomplishment.

The best time to create a list is either at the beginning of the day or at its end, in preparation for the next day. Your list will develop from two sources. The first source consists of those tasks that have devolved from your activities during the day which you need to address either the next day or soon after. The second source is your daily calendar, review of our rescheduled important items that you need to act on.

As your life becomes more complex, the daily "to do" list will get longer. Implementing these few minor organizational strategies will save you time and effort. First, group similar tasks together and do them all at once. For example, in one sitting, you can make all your phone calls; open and read e-mail, pay bills or take care of correspondence. In other words, group the tasks together that can be intermingled because of their natural relationship.

This kind of planning is even more important when you're out running errands. Make as few trips as you can and plan the most efficient route. When out shopping, don't forget to have a list of everything you need so you don't have to make an additional trip for forgotten items.

One of the most important organizational strategies you can use is very simple: finish one task before you start another. Of course sometimes a project is so extensive that it can't be finished in one session. In those cases, break the project down into smaller steps, then systematically complete each step before you move on to the next. For example, gathering research papers, reading and translating them into note cards, and writing a first draft of the paper are natural steps for completing the larger task of writing a term paper. You work on the larger project a little at a time, always making progress through the completion of the larger project.

Organize the Academic Period

If organizing the daily schedule provides the close-up picture, organizing the quarter or semester gives one a panoramic view. The goals are similar to those in organizing your day. This will keep you on track with the needs of the entire academic period. This broader scope of organization allows you to establish priorities and set deadlines within the big picture of everything you need to accomplish during a quarter or semester. The starting point for this organizational plan comes during the first week of school, when course outlines, which include papers, tests and other expected work for class, are given. When you receive all of the course syllabi, you're ready to start developing the big picture of your tasks for the quarter or semester.

Remember that large calendar, I suggested you buy, the one with lots of room for you to write on for each day? Take a calendar or write down all of the test dates, term paper due dates, project due dates. You want anything with a deadline that you must meet. A brightly colored fluorescent highlighter makes the task really stand out on a calendar; color coding the tasks is even more helpful. You will put much of the same information in your day timer so you have a portable version of the larger one. Visual reminders are powerful ways to keep on track. Having duplication is worth the extra effort.

The same master calendar strategy readily translates to life in a family where everyone has their own needs and commitments. For any major time commitment or appointment that will impact others n the family, it all goes on the master calendar. The plethora of soccer practices, dentist appointments and social activities. Next, break down larger tasks into their natural, smaller steps and assign a completion date for each of these steps. For papers, you will need to gather reference materials, read and process articles, and write a final draft. To alleviate the pressure of deadlines, assign a completion date at least one week prior to the due date. This can save you a great deal of stress, and with the widespread availability of computers, you should be able to make any last-minute corrections or additions that may grow out of the lecture.

Preparing for a test essentially takes the same path as the steps involved in writing a paper. Break down the larger job of preparing for a test into smaller, more manageable tasks. Here are a few questions which will help you get organized;

- How many times you need to review material for a particular course to prepare for the test?
- Do the lectures depend on you having completed the reading? If this is the case, schedule your reading time before the lecture.
- Are you going to have a study session with others? These too can be scheduled at the beginning of the academic.

Schedule some time on the day before a test for an overall review of the material to be covered. Don't leave this last and most important task until the day of the exam. Last-minute cramming is not nearly as effective as they methodically developed process of study, and it can make you feel rushed and anxious. When you maintain your steady, step-by-step study plan, you are more focused and retain information better.

When should you plan on studying for a particular course? The answer is: before the lecture. This may sound strange, but it goes back to the idea of clumping similar tasks together. You read the material, and then you hear the professor lecture on the same material. These complementary strategies make the learning more integrated as ideas from the reading are echoed in the lecture. A higher degree of retention and comprehension is possible because the material becomes anchored in multiple representational systems -in this case visual than auditory.

I suggest adding what and when you plan to study to that big calendar. Again, use distinctive colors, ones that are different from those you've already used to designate exams and papers. At this point, the organization of the term starts to really tighten up and take shape; you can see exactly what shall be doing as you progress through your courses. Remember, all this organization is merely a tool to help keep you on track to make consistent progress toward a particular goal.

While organizational strategies for writing term papers or preparing for tests have many similarities, they also have some important differences. Tests measure a student's mastery and recall of information presented a number of times, particularly during a series of lectures. A term paper reflects the student's ability to develop and integrate related information often gathered outside of the lecture. The steps requiring in preparing for a test are frequent and repetitious in nature. Steps taken to write a paper are usually not repetitive, but more extensive in nature.

Consider a different approach to integrating two level of preparation. During the week (Sunday through Thursday), I focused on the lecture in test preparation, which allowed me to take advantage of linking the course reading with the lecture. On the weekend (Friday through Sunday), I put the weekly materials aside and focus on paper preparation, taking advantage of the fact that the library was less crowded during these times. Of course, I found there were times I couldn't stick to the schedule, and being flexible as important. For the most part, the separation of tasks worked very well, but had some added in advantage in alleviating the feeling that I had to do everything at once.

Use the calendar feature on your personal computer to produce calendars for each course of the academic. Place a calendar with test and paper due dates in the front of each course is note book for that quarter. This provided an additional and handy reminder for the demands of a particular course. Visual repetition reinforces tracking of important tasks and dates.

While organizational strategies are important in addressing the demands of school, there are a number of easy, straightforward ways of saving time and becoming more efficient -info for school and life.

Top Ten Time-Savers for Academic Efficiency

1. Use your waiting time! The day is full of spaces of time where you must wait. It doesn't have to be lost time. Get in the habit of carrying something with you to read. I often reviewed flashcards during the downtime between periods of hockey games. Whether its flashcards or a book or lecture notes, keep something you need to read handy. Not only will you put that otherwise wasted time to use, you lessen the frustration that comes with having to wait.

2. Minimize schmoozing time! It is easy to get distracted by friends, especially when you're looking for an excuse not to do work. Social time offers an important component to keeping your life balance, but you don't want it to interfere with your study time. The solution is to combine your socializing with lunch and dinner breaks. When you do this, the time you spend with your friends becomes valuable, and high quality time. Making a lunch or dinner date with friends gives you something to look forward to, and the rewards for your hard work. The conversation will not only provide you with a needed break from your studies, it will actually help you slow down your eating, which makes a meal more enjoyable and healthy. When I share a meal with friends, we make it a rule to talk about something other than our work or our studies. We focus on just enjoying one another's company. I always come away feeling relaxed, renewed, and ready to go back to work.

3. Schedule your recreational time. The old saying "All work and no play makes Jack a dull boy" is true. It's easily to get so consumed by exams, projects or papers that we neglect our important relationships. Planning to spend time in enjoyable pursuits, with your family or by yourself is fundamental to sustaining yourself through the rigors

of academic life. Recreational activities will leave you feeling refreshed and rejuvenated, much like recharging a battery. It will also help your school work into proper perspective. Failing to make time to relax and have fun is a sure prescription for burnout and resentment of school in the process of education. Aerobic exercise is a physiologic way of increasing focus. Prior to writing, I will spend time on the rowing machine. Pick-up basketball was something that was part of my early routine. Forty-five minutes to an hour of playing hoops, a quick dinner and you will find yourself far more dialed in to sitting at a desk working.

4. Prevent needless interruptions. Stick a sign on your door that says you are not available until a specific time, such as 10 p.m. Use your voicemail like a secretary. Let it take up the calls, you can screen them, leaving all but the most urgent calls until later. Turn the ringer off of the phone while you're studying. There is no sense sitting and wondering who just called you. The tendency will be to check this and then distract yourself from the task at hand.

5. Study when you are at peak efficiency. This is one that is really worth focusing on. Don't try to work late into the night after a long hard day. It's far better to get up earlier the next morning and put in some study time at the beginning of the day when you are fresh. Determine what time in the evening is a good time to stop for you. That time before going bed can be used to wind down and return social calls.

6. Limit your time watching television. Use TV for wind down time, not as your main form of recreation or as an excuse to avoid your studies. There is nothing on TV as important as creating your future by successfully advancing your education. If there is something you really must see, the technology is there to record it and watch it later.

7. Invest in the tools to properly do the job at hand. Although the initial cost is higher than you might like, you will find it to be money well spent. The right tools will save you time

and effort. Have good comfortable chair that fits your body size. It must provide enough physical comfort to remain in it for a couple of hours. Don't skimp on lighting. I advised a combination of incandescent and florescent. Not all materials are printed with paper and type that is ideal. Different types of like will ease eye strain.

8. Use those services available that will help you produce a better product and less time. One example that I particularly like, is voice recognition technology. This book has largely been written using that technology. I am at best, a very poor typist. Not only can I dictate at 120 words per minute, my voice recognition technology is a far better speller than I am. The downside is that that technology is not perfect. You will get some interesting miss reads on what you have said. If I put any monetary value on my time, purchasing this particular program has paid for itself many times over. Graduate students often provide critiquing and proofreading papers for a fee. Some schools will pick up the tab for this service as part of accommodations under the Americans with Disabilities Act. These people can often be found through the department secretary, other students or on a school bulletin board.

9. Many professors seem to suffer from the delusion that their course is the only thing, or certainly the most important thing, that you have going on in your life. In an attempt to share all that there is to know on the subject, they will assign an overwhelming amount of reading. You can't always predict which Professor will do this. The number of credits per course may be a poor indicator of the amount of reading in preparation for that course. As always, a student should endeavor to read whatever material or professor has assigned. When you find yourself faced with more reading than you can possibly manage, try this strategy. For all the recommended readings, read the first paragraph of the piece. This will introduce the overall subject. Follow this by reading the first sentence

of each successive paragraph. This will identify key points. This summary may be the most useful part of a piece of paper, in that it will reiterate the relevant and significant points of the material. This nicely forms the basis for a review card to add to your latter study. When I made a quick reference to some of the extra reading in a course in an essay question on a test, the instructor wrote in large letters, "I can see you're really on top of things." The reality was that I thought essay should have been rated a 'B'. That little addition pushed it to an 'A'.

10. Organize your work and living space. Messes are not just efficient, they are tiring. If instilling organization means you are faced with large-scale revamping of your living spaces, start with areas that bother you the most. Do a little bit every day; even if you clear off just one tabletop, you've taken a step toward getting the job done. You will reap the benefit of the neat and orderly environment.

Reality Check: Even though I know what to do to get and keep my life organized, my desk gets messy. I will have times when clutter gets the best of me. What you are trying to do is learn new ways of doing things and then build good habits around those skills. As a therapist and a coach, I believe in the power of reward. Take two or three of these suggestions. Enact them in your life for a week. At the end of the week, give yourself a small reward. I like things that would be considered self nurturing. If it's something you do anyway, then it is not a new reward. Just before you give yourself your reward, have a moment to reflect on why you're reinforcing the work to make change.

The world at large is remarkably poor at giving us positive strokes for our efforts to change and succeed at pushing out growing edges of our life. The very worst jobs are ones where employees get no feedback about their efforts. A close second is work where only the negative is brought to one's attention.

As a therapist, what I want to foster is an internal sense of acknowledgement for a person's efforts. How many of us that played some sort of sports don't recall the power of coach or perhaps another team mates telling us we did a good job? If we count on the external world to do this for us, then we will find ourselves disappointed. Moving reinforcement to an internal process leads to a point where we can feel good about what we do, even if no one else notices it.

Balance

Even with the best laid plans in our lives do not often follow our agenda. Our families are seldom working from the same game plan that we are. Children have an especially difficult time understanding that the parent is too busy to spend time with them. They often suffer hurt and disappointment, and can sometimes perceive this as abandonment. The other side of the coin is one of the parent-student finding themselves overburdened. There never seems to be enough time for both study time, earning a living, and their family responsibilities. It is natural to become resentful and short tempered with interruptions.

The irony is that rigidly sticking to an agenda can set us up to generate more pressure than is necessary. From the perspective of a child, a parent who is inflexible, who must stick to their plan no matter what, makes them appear unavailable and without response into the child's needs. Children will often hide their disappointment, but act out in anger. This behavior is an accurate barometer for the tension that a parent is experiencing.

An agenda should be viewed as a guide or an ideal of what you want to accomplish. Childhood doesn't wait. Special moments pass an instant and are forever lost, if not experienced when they happen. There are of course times when we must get a certain amount of work done. You must have time when you're fully present and focused on your work. The same applies to having time where you are fully present with the important people in your life.

Creating a balance in your life will continue with the demands of school is a difficult task. You may want to plan starting your day with high-quality time with your family. This can be as simple as sitting down to breakfast together. Negotiate the time you need to do your work. Think about a way of finishing up your day with the people you care about.

School is not the end-all, or the be-all of life. It is a transition time. Inner balance comes from maintaining contact with people in our lives who sustain us. Learning how to be flexible and let go of a rigid agenda allows us to stay contact with what is truly meaningful in our lives. A belief in writing this book is that if we lose the relationships with the people most important to us, it does not matter what letters are now placed behind your name. You have not succeeded. Organization is a tool that should help us accomplish our goals. It should never be our master.

·9·

Self Care: Keeping the Mind and Body Well Tuned

The body is an instrument, the mind its function,
the witness and reward of its operation.
-*George Santayana*

I finally realized that by being grateful to my body
was key to giving more love to myself.
-*Oprah Winfrey*

The mind and the body share a powerful relationship. The mind is the directing force in the use of the body. The health and well-being of our physical being influences the brain's ability to function. Physical fatigue decreases mental acuity. It hampers the mind's ability to think clearly and to filter stimuli from the environment. Think of a driver with a car whose steering wheel keeps pulling to one side. The driver has to expend so much effort and concentration on just keeping the car on the road that his attention is diverted from other important aspects of driving. He may fail to notice traffic signs, or watch for oncoming cars. It is only a matter of time before an accident occurs.

The student who is physically tired suffers from all sorts of obstacles to study. It becomes difficult to concentrate. The need to reread material increases. Writing ceases to flow easily. Task persistence is reduced. Physical fatigue leaves us less motivated to gear a fundamental effort and demand for performing the tasks that school requires. Thoughts wander and getting started doing our work is delayed. The mind justifies a few minutes of settling down before hitting the books. This time draws out and easily becomes a more extended period of time. People with an ADD/ADHD frequently have a very poor sense of the passage of time. When the student finally sits down to accomplish the task at hand, anxiety over where the time has gone can sap creativity. Higher mental processes either shut down or function so poorly that it becomes a struggle to create. Many artists and writers purposely planned their creative work in the morning, since this is when they are most rested.

The way to manage physical and mental fatigue is to simply get adequate sleep. Of course, the pressure of school can push you to study long after you become tired. If you have deadlines to meet, you are afraid that you don't know the material as well as you should. You feel overwhelmed and afraid you can't get it all done. There comes a point where the cost of continuing to study exceeds the benefits. There is no point in sacrificing your rest when you can't use the time to study at your optimum.

The answer is to study at times when you feel you can do so most effectively. The retention of information depends more on the quality rather than the quantity of study. Don't expect to remember material well when you're really beat. It just won't happen. I suggest using the early hours of the day for strenuous mental activity, such as studying, and saving the less demanding tasks for later. It's time to develop the ability to be able to say to yourself, "That's enough for one day."

Sleep

Sleep is the body's way of recharging its batteries. How much sleep do we really need to be truly rested? The amount will vary during your lifetime. Factors such as age, physical and mental output, diet, exercise are all factors. Most people will need about eight hours of sleep. This is a medium amount. Some people feel fully rested after five to six hours; others need nine or more hours. Current research suggests that the minimum amount of sleep necessary for a 24 hour period is four to five hours. If we fall below that, task performance suffers greatly. The right amount of sleep for you is that which leaves you feeling fully alert through the course of the day.

Our change in lifestyle over the last few decades is altered our sleep. At the turn of the century, most people got an average of nine hours of sleep. This coincides loosely to the hours of daylight in nighttime. Sleepiness is influenced by circadian rhythms which are light mediated. In the past when there were fewer options for entertainment, people went to bed when it got dark. Today we compress more into our everyday life. We often participate in activities well into the night time. At the end of a long day, we often watch television, which competes with sleep time. People in North America and Japan work more hours than people anywhere else in the world. As days and weeks of this lifestyle wear on, sleep deprivation becomes cumulative. Researchers describe this process as "sleep debt". This is a mounting charge on the bodies account that they will eventually need to be paid. You don't necessarily have to make up for every hour of sleep loss. Most people will catch up if they are allowed to sleep for two consecutive nights where sleep is open ended, and you do not wake to an alarm clock. For night shift workers, the problem is worse. Working the night shift distorts the person circadian rhythm. Many students work night shifts to accommodate their schedules at school. This can be a benefit in allowing for large blocks of time with which to study. The price paid in maintaining this kind of schedule is that recovery time will take longer. It may be three to four days before full daytime alertness and mental acuity is achieved. The recovery period may be filled with frequent waking. The student who must work nights should group work shifts and days off as much as possible. This limits the number of times you have to turn around your wake-sleep pattern.

If you choose, or if you are required to work night shifts, do it part-time if at all possible. This will allow more time to catch up on sleep and the "payoff" of your sleep debt. Work that requires you to be mentally clear, such as studying must be put off until the time when you have recovered from working nights.

Most of us experience difficulty in sleeping from time to time. For the person with ADD/ADHD difficulty falling asleep is often a problem. For some people it is simply hard to turn one's mind off at the end of a day. Using a distraction like watching television or reading until one is overcome by fatigue, and finally does fall asleep in is an unfortunate strategy. About 10-15% of the adults that I treat for ADD/ADHD benefit from a small dose of a short acting stimulant, just before bed as a means of going to sleep. The wiring for an ADD/ADHD brain is different. Using a stimulate to go to sleep seems counter-intuitive. Low dose stimulants can make people with ADD/ADHD sleepy. This accounts for some of the fatigue when using long-acting stimulants and having a medication holiday where you choose not to use medications.

·10·
Putting Yourself to the Test

*I was always looking outside myself for strength
and confidence, but it comes from within. It is
there all the time.*
-Anna Freud

Evaluation of the student's mastery of the courses' information is a fact of academic life. Instructors assess the learner's proficiency in a number of ways: presentations, papers, participation in class discussion, and of course, formal testing. While a grade is an important measure of learning, too often it becomes a goal unto itself, overshadowing the original goal of personal mastery of the information. If a student approaches their education from a perspective of wanting to understand, use, and truly master the information the teacher has to give, then the grades will follow.

If you are a person with ADD/ADHD who is entering college right from high school and after having lived in your parent's house, you will now be faced with setting your own schedule. You will have to push and prompt yourself to get your homework done and meet a class schedule on your own instead of having your folks there to take that role.

The passage of time is frequently very different for the person with ADD/ADHD. Time can both creep and leap. For the person with ADD/ADHD, there can be major difficulties in estimating the time required for assignments. The sequential planning of the steps needed to complete a project can be problematic. Homework may seem to take forever and lead to avoidance as a consequence of distractibility. How many times do you sit down to study or do an assignment without checking e-mail, text messages, and an assortment of other distractions? Yes, you have been busy. This is by no means the same as being productive. It is not a badge of honor to be able to say that you spent thirty hours at your desk working on a project. It bespeaks the fact that you are likely busy but not productive.

Focusing only on getting a good grade is a sort of pressure and may fuel your activity. Corporations often use transcripts as a measure of the candidate's inherent abilities. Class standing has a direct correlation to future income in a number of different fields. Access to future education is often determined by grade point average. The higher the level of degree, the more competition there will be among students for access to that education. Entry into those high demand programs will depend on previous academic success. Doing well in school is always desirable. The skills needed to glean the most out of education are the same skills used to successfully navigate within the realm of formal evaluation.

In discussing ways of becoming a better student, I want to share a concept with you. It comes from Vilfredo Pareto, an Italian economist who was born in 1848. He noticed that 80% of the land was owned by 20% of the population. He found that in most situations, given numbers greater than fifty, 20% will account for most of the resources or the best grades. He extrapolated this to form the concept of "Praedo's Optimality" and "Pareto's Efficiency." In the world of academia, twenty percent of a class will excel. When it comes to your own work, twenty percent of your efforts will yield 80% of your results. Where does this begin? With you, of course!

Winning Attitude. Being in Paredo's Top 20%.

Demand as much from yourself as you demand from your professor. I went to a school that had a professor who is regarded as one of the national leaders in the field of alcohol studies. He wrote an excellent book on the subject. Unfortunately during the class, all he did was regurgitate the book. Since I was paying for my education myself, I decided to figure out just what it costs me to be in his class. (This is an interesting exercise and a big help if you're considering whether one of your classes might be expendable). At a small, private university, I figured out the amount I was paying for each class. For that kind of money I was spending, I wanted more than what I could get on my own by reading the book. After all, I had the opportunity to learn directly from the nationally regarded expert.

When I confronted the professor that I wanted more than just the content of his book, I had to come to grips with my part of the relationship. If I was going to demand more from my instructor, I had to be ready to demand more for myself. For every student, that starts with class time.

Think of it as an opportunity. To take advantage of any chance life offers, you must be adequately prepared. Always complete your assigned reading prior to coming to class. If you don't, then you rely on hearing the material "cold". You may find yourself lost. You want your classroom time to be focused on active learning. When you come prepared, what you gain from your reading is reinforced and pushed to a higher level by the discussion in class.

Develop a "heads up" attitude about participating in class. Get to class on time. Return from breaks on time. In nursing school, I had an instructor who closed and locked the door would break time was over. If you didn't make it back on time, too bad, you lost out. What this instructor demanded was the same level of professionalism about school that is demanded in the working world. The habits and attitudes you develop while in school directly translate to the same factors you will need to excel in your career.

Overcome "first row--itis." Whenever there are plenty of seats for students, the first row in the classroom will often remain vacant. Notice where the best students tend to sit. They tend to be seated close to the instructor. Those who aren't doing as well are found in the back half of the classroom. You want to be one of those students fighting for a seat in front! Where else are you going to be able to see and hear things best?

The front row is the least distracting place to sit. This is particularly important for the ADD/ADHD student. If you are in a mega-class with 500 to a thousand students, the importance of keeping the crowd behind you is amplified. When you sit in the front, you stay more alert. You have a sense of direct contact with your instructor. You are less likely to let your thoughts drift. For many people with ADD/ADHD information is received and processed better if you can see a person's lips move. This allows their input to come in both auditory and visual pathways.

In the mega-class scenario, sitting in the front will give you other advantages. The instructor and a mega-class can only make eye contact with those people sitting in the front. The rest of the class becomes an impersonal sea of faces. When you sit in the front, the professor is more likely to know your name and view you on a more personal level. You convey that you are there to learn and take an active role in class.

In smaller classes and study groups, discussion becomes the focal point. Be ready to actively engage in the synergy of minds. This is where you will develop a higher level of understanding and mastery. Discussion acts as a catalyst in developing new and different perspectives on the subject that will give you the opportunity to develop critical thinking skills. The intellectual stimulation that exchange of ideas provokes can be one of the best rewards of an academic experience. Many people with ADD/ADHD can recall information more readily in this format. I have had many clients say that they would be a great student if they just didn't have to take tests. Changing format from multiple choice questions to essay is an accommodation that sometimes is granted. It can be better way for the ADD/ADHD student to demonstrate their knowledge. In classes with discussion, many ADD/ADHD students find their opportunity to shine. Passion and ideas often mix leaving you contemplating course material, long after classes ended. When you can achieve that level and type of stimulation, memory and subsequent recall for exams becomes far easier.

Shifting the Paradigm to 20% of Effort leading to 80% of Results

The sheer volume of some textbooks can leave you feeling buried before you even open them up. To keep from being overwhelmed, remember that task of the student is not to read every word, but to separate the essence of the material.

The core material is what the teacher will use to build an exam. Core material from the hard sciences may be largely fact and formula based. High-fact volume situations require repetition to learn. It is ideally suited to a flash card format for repeated reviews of the material. Foundation materials from the humanities can include concepts, theories, and people and events of note. This information can be adapted to a flash card strategy too. When you first open the textbook, examine its layout. Many books are formatted to assist you in pulling out the most important material. If your text has a chapter outline, the essence of the core material is served to you on a platter. Start making flashcards with each heading title. Arrange them in sequential order of the chapter outline. These are guideposts of the reading, telling you what to expect as you journey through the chapter.

As you begin your reading, notice how the sections start with the main idea or concept. You want to pull out the "what, why, and how." This is where you pull out the significance of concepts. On your flash card, state the essential facts or information about the basic concept. You can skim the rest of the section for supporting data. This allows you to cover a lot of reading material in a short amount of time.

Highlighting can help the process. Curb the urge to highlight more than you need to, as it will only diminish its usefulness. For highlighting to be effective, it must be to "highlight" just the important facts. Take the same approach as you would to making a flash card. The basic concept is all that should be highlighted. This is usually only about 10% of the information. You may want to experiment with highlighting before making flashcards. It is quicker to highlight them to write something down. You may find this more efficient as a way for you to move through the reading, and as a way of quickly making your review cards.

Books that do not have a chapter outline are a bit more difficult. They can be approached in essentially the same way. As you begin a chapter, take a few minutes to go through and write down the section headings. These become a roadmap for the chapter. Headings separate out various clusters of information. You can use them to title information on your flashcards. For sections that have multiple concepts, principles, people or events, titles group related information.

Dialing in Pareto's Efficiency: Construction of Memory

Marketing theory tells us that we need at least seven repetitions to remember a name or a fact. Large corporations spend vast amounts of their advertising budget to bombard us with information about their products. We retained relevant information. How many of us can readily tell what companies advertising goes with an inane advertising jingle. It is a factor of repetition.

Ever wonder why a 14-year-old can have a photographic memory for statistics of a player on his favorite team, yet constantly forget to take out the garbage? A stimulus driven brain is attracted to and recalls information that it finds appealing. Unfortunately, we are required to recall things which may not have great inherent appeal. For us to really seat the information to long-term memory and develop full recall, repetition is an essential element.

When you study, your first repetition of material comes from making flashcards during your initial reading of the material. This is a first step to analyzing the information and breaking it down into meaningful concepts and relationships.

Your second review occurs fairly soon after you complete your reading. Take a short break in between. Stretch. Go get your circulation going again. Wash your face. Enjoy a refreshing drink. Your goal is to clear your head. Now you're ready to take on the second pass on the information. After you complete this, you'll be ready to actively participate in classroom discussion.

Think of the second pass through on material as digestion. Once you've ingested the information, now you want to see if it makes sense. Do the supporting facts actually support the concepts are principles? If you are learning about a particular person or event, think of why and how the person or events is important? You want to illustrate how the information may be relevant, on either a personal or professional level. Your goal is to develop an interest that motivates you to invest in long-term recall by finding its relevancy to your own life.

Here is a case in point: Why would a construction manager need to study basic psychology? The subjects of psychology and construction seem pretty far removed from one another. What if the study of psychology to give the construction manager different and effective tools to increase productivity and reliability? What if applying certain psychological principles, you could create an environment within the company that would make employees want to stay, and feel invested in the product the company creates? Let's take the psychological concepts that a variable schedule and variable amount for enforcement is extremely powerful. It is the concept by which casinos rake in huge profits. It asserts that by giving rewards intermittently and in varying amounts, a certain behavior can be established. This type of reinforcement is the most powerful type of reinforcement. The construction manager puts the principle into practice by awarding bonuses in variable amounts on an intermittent basis. The utility of applied psychology now has relevance to the manager's life. For students, particularly in introductory classes, it can be very difficult to find relevance of interest. Finding your own use for a concept is a key element in anchoring long-term recall.

The third review is to make comments during class, particularly if the class has discussion is a daily part of its format. Bring your flashcards to class. Before information is seated into your long-term memory, flashcards can provide you with a quick reference to facts and concepts. This can make your contribution to discussion more powerful. When you reference the information from your cards, you make a strong statement to your professor. You are perceived as a person who is not only prepared, but has developed insights about the subject matter. You have identified yourself as a high-level student. You further anchor information into long term memory.

This third pass during class time is where you start to integrate information. Your hearing more about what you've covered in the reading. You can draw in the expertise of the instructed to clarify and expound on the written information. If you ask a question class, it demands integrated recall. The result is start cementing information into long term memory. That level of engagement enhances learning in a very powerful way. When you have publicly asked a question, a physical response occurs that is kinesthetically linked to the information. The concepts you struggle most with are the very things you want to clarify by questioning, either during or after class. You'll find that repetitions after the third pass become quicker as the material becomes increasingly familiar. Reviews become a building process as you continually add more information.

On the day of the exam, leave your cards at home. There is a tendency to want to do one more last review prior to taking in the exam. Last-minute reviews can do more to increase anxiety rather than help you recall the information. If you have had between 10 and 20 repetitions of the information, YOU WILL RECALL THE INFORMATION! For extremely fact dense subjects like anatomy, you may find that you need more repetitions to retain the vast quantity of information. The saving grace of high levels of repetition is that each time you go through your cards, you pick up speed.

Recall of formulas requires a somewhat different approach to using the tool of repetition. If your text has test sample questions at the end of the chapter, by all means, take advantage of them. Make up your own sample questions and use them for practice. Sororities or fraternities generally have test files of previous exams. These can be an abundant source of potential questions. You may find some of the questions from old exams are found on the current test.

In the medical profession, there is a teaching axiom: See one, do one, teach one. The "See one" phase is your first exposure to the information. "Do one" refers to take in information and applying it in a variety of situations. This may be making several simple math problems to solve, as a means of gaining experience using a formula. The "teach one" phase is the part that most effectively locks and information in the vault of long-term memory.

Teaching is an excellent way to integrate and become adept using information. How can you teach someone to use a formula question? Become a tutor or present information in a study group. If your level of understanding develops to a point where you can teach others, you have fine-tuned your own understanding of the subject.

Dialing in Pareto's Efficiency: Attack Strategies

Imagine for a moment that you are a professional athlete who must perform tomorrow in a big game. If you went out the night before, had a few drinks, and didn't get to bed until very late, would you expect your performance to be the best on the next day? Of course not!

As a student preparing for exams, you are no different in this respect from a professional athlete preparing for again. Your first test strategy is to get enough rest so you are at your sharpest.

Eating well is an important means of preparation. You will have less physical distraction from hunger, and get the energy to boost your performance. Be aware of the effect of carbohydrates in the afternoon. The last thing you want to do is fight the natural wish to take a nap during a test.

On exam day come to class a little early. Nothing adds to anxiety like having to rush to class and jump into an exam. What you're taking a test, you want to focus on exactly what each question is asking. Take enough time that you are sure you know, what is being asked. You may want to use a highlighter to help focus on the essence of the question. By being thorough in this approach, you illuminate the common problem of having to change answers as you review the test. When you take the time to read and understand the question adequately the first time you see it, you save yourself a lot of time and trouble.

Understanding Strategy and Structure
Deductive Reasoning and Objective Tests

Objective tests (true-false or multiple-choice), are the norm for larger classes. It is just too time-consuming for an instructor to approach evaluation in any other way. They are also the easiest type of tests to take. Objective tests require recognition rather than recollection, or synthesis. Recognition of what is familiar is a much simpler task than the integration of information required in synthesis. They are also the type of test which requires the simplest strategy to determine the answer to the question.

Look for keywords particularly words that denote an absolute. All, none, every, never, always, and nothing all indicate an absolute. In most fields of study, there are very few absolutes. "All absolutes are false," is in itself an absolute. It is a good role of thumb is to remember that if the question is framed as an absolute, it will most likely be false.

One trap for true-false questions is to pair a true statement with an incorrect one. The statement is quickly read, the true part jumps out to the test taker. The false part of the question may involve a lesser-known factor piece of information. The student, responding to the fact known to be true, is often deceived in making the wrong choice. As tantalizing as the true part is, anything recognized as false eliminates that answer.

Multiple-choice questions mix recognition with deductive strategies. Using deductive strategies, you can readily chew through the multiple-choice exam. First read the question. Are you sure you know what it is asking? Are you able to identify responses that are definitely false? You can cross every answer out that contains something false. The corollary to this is generally true as well. You recognize the fact is true. It will more than likely indicate the correct answer. Using recognition as a technique helps you reduce the odds of choosing the incorrect answer.

What if you find yourself reading and rereading a question, either because you don't know the answer, or you're just plain stuck? There is a danger in over reading. You can interpret more than what is being asked in the question here is where use of a highlighter can be beneficial. Highlight the essence of the question, and don't get bogged down and let anxiety build by struggling with a particular question. Mark the question for return and move through the test. The answer may be sparked by content from another question. In that case go back and make your selection. If no thunderbolts or insights strike you, wait until you are done with the rest of the exam before going back.

Some professors will allow students to use highlighters in the course of their exams. I will often put this as a specific accommodation requested when I do an accommodations petition under the Americans with Disabilities Act. It is a strategy that allows the student to use multiple pathways for understanding information.

Essay Questions

A difficulty for the student with ADD/ADHD is holding events or information in one's mind. This is a temporal lobe difficulty with impairment of internalizing language. When I given a client medication instructions, I am mindful of providing the person with written instructions as well as verbal ones. This executive function leads to problems taking the whole apart and reconstituting. People with ADD/ADHD often have poor listening and reading comprehension. I had several professors who would test in a rather free form way and verbally explain what they wanted you to write about for your exam. Obtaining written test instructions is an accommodation you may wish your advocate to petition for.

Several other difficulties exist for the student with ADD/ADHD. It is often hard to describe the world in words. With slower retrieval of information, written expression can be more problematic. Efficiency in understanding what is being asked saves time and allows you to dial in on content. Untimed tests are another accommodation that is quite helpful for the ADD/ADHD student.

A first step is to really understand the structure of essay questions. Essay questions come in two types: descriptive and analytical. Answering either kind begins with careful reading of the question. Be sure, you know what the question is asking. If the instructor gives directions to address particular facet of the question, then highlight those to make sure that they are in your essay. Write the type of essay asked for, be it descriptive or analytical in the margin or use a highlighter to draw visual attention to key words in the question.

A second step for both descriptive and analytical essay questions is to form a brief outline for your response. The descriptive is by far the easiest in this regard. Your responses grow directly out of the information on the flashcards you been studying. You should be readily able to recall the "why" and the "how" of the people and events that you study. The integrated part of your preparation allows you to explain the impact of the events and concepts you have studied.

Comparing or contrasting pieces of information is a further evolution of the descriptive essay. If your professor asks for a particular type essay question, then tailor the information in your flashcards to show a connection between two or more events. The quick outline meant you write enables you to identify similarities and differences.

The analytic essay question requires a synthesis of facts. The instructor may have you defend a particular point of view rather than let you choose which side of an argument you would like to make a case for. Whether you are given a predetermined point of view, or allowed to choose your own, you must construct a logical argument by presenting facts which lead to your conclusion. This is where an outline is indispensable. The outline becomes the structure of your logic. You save time and are more efficient and effective in presenting your argument if you first construct a short outline. You can flesh out your own thoughts as you write the essay. The outline allows you to identify simple cause-and-effect relationships or build a case for your conclusions.

If you have been an active participant in classroom discussion, the experience will come in handy when responding to this type of question. Synthesis of ideas is a natural outcome of discussion. This process will come to you, naturally, if you practice it in a classroom setting. Again, a brief outline will help you formulate your thoughts and stay focused.

Your essay outline should have a common format should define the problem, be it a comparison or contrast. Note your position or the one the instructor has asked you to write about. The body of the outline bullet points supporting facts. End the outline with 'Summary'. Why is your conclusion important? What is its impact or relevance? Draw your conclusion and close. Rambling on is a tendency and a trap easily fallen into by people with ADD/ADHD. You outline can help you write a focused essay, that is clear and to the point.

Test Anxiety

You arrive on time for the mid-term exam and you find yourself a seat. Suddenly, you become aware that your hands are moist and your pulse races. As you wait for the test papers to be handed out, your anxiety grows. You attempt to recall simple facts from your pretest studying and draw a complete blank on material you clearly know. Negative thoughts begin to creep in until you are truly nearing catatonia. "I am going to fail," you tell yourself. The negative emotional thoughts become increasingly irrational and destructive. You think, "everyone is going to know that I am a failure." When you finally get the test paper and you reach your first question, your mind seems completely empty as you struggle to think of where to begin. Your chest tightens, making it difficult to breathe. You have to fight just to stay in the room and complete the exam.

Is this an unrealistic scenario? Not at all. Test anxiety affects the student on a physical, emotional and cognitive level. It may escalate into full-blown episodes of terror, not unlike the process that occurs in panic disorders. Relatively benign thoughts or physical sensations are interpreted catastrophically leading to an intensifying cycle where the anxious fears begin to feed on themselves. For the person with ADD/ADHD, it is common for anxiety to be performance driven. Taking test can be a powerful trigger to feeling anxious. The intervention is fairly simple, has no side effects save for a sense of well being and costs only time for practice. The benefits translate to other situations as well.

Since it is impossible to be anxious and relaxed at the same time, the first task and effectively dealing with test anxiety as to interrupt that the debilitating physical component. You can do this by practicing a simple technique called the "quieting breath." This exercise should take no more than eight to 10 seconds. You will find that it works well for all types of anxiety, particularly performance anxiety. The advantage is that it can be done both quickly and is effective in a wide variety of settings.

Exercise #1

First, close your eyes. Draw in a slow deep breath to a slow count to four, then hold it for one or two seconds. Breathe out to a count of four, and hold your breath again, for one to two seconds. During the pause as you will notice a brief sense of inner calm, often described as stillness in your chest. Repeat as often as you feel you need to do so.

The quieting breath may be enough for you to interrupt the developing anxiety. Sometimes slightly more extensive techniques may need to be employed. In 1928, Edmund Jacobson, M.D., wrote a book called Progressive Relaxation (1). In this book, Jacobson was the first to explore the effect of tension on physical health and to develop a practical method of taking conscious control over muscular tension.

His technique called "progressive relaxation," shows how to identify where a person holds muscular tension. The individual undertakes a progressive sequence of first tensing, and then relaxing various muscle groups. After being held under tension, a muscle fiber lengthens or relaxes to a greater extent than it did prior to being held in a contracted, or tense state. This method teaches the person to identify the feeling within their muscles in a relaxed state, and contrast them with the feeling of muscle tension. Eventually a person learns how to release tension without having to go through the process of tensing then relaxing each and every muscle group.

Is true with any skill, progressive relaxation becomes easier with practice. Full-length scripts of progressive relaxation techniques are available from a variety of sources, including the internet. Regular daily practice, aside from being fun and relaxing, it is required to gain mastery of the scale. The following is a brief, modified progressive will relaxation technique for use prior to taking an exam.

Exercise #2

Start by closing your eyes and taking a slow, relaxed breath as described in Exercise #1. Are there parts of your body that feel tense, even painful? Where are they? Tilting your head back slightly, shrug your shoulders tightly and hold that shrug for 5-10 seconds. Repeat this step once more. Slowly turn your head to the side stretching the muscles in your night. Repeat this in the opposite direction. Wrap your arms around her upper torso so that your hands touched her shoulder blades. If you can't reach your shoulder blades, come as close as you can. Slowly twist to one direction and hold for five seconds. Repeat this step in the opposite direction. With your arm still wrapped around your upper torso, drop your chin to your chest and curl your upper body forward. Notice how much looser you feel. This can be complicated by massaging yourself on the neck and shoulders. These steps can be repeated as many times as you feel necessary.

Progress to the lower body, bring your knees up to your chest. This will stretch out your lower back (wear pants for this one!).

Another technique for conquering test anxiety is cognitive

interruption. This occurs before you meet the challenge of an exam. Every situation or event in our lives is influenced by our beliefs. Beliefs can be described as "a strong emotional and cognitive state of certainty." Given the same event, individuals will respond differently based on their beliefs. When overcome with test anxiety, our beliefs often turned negative, with irrational thoughts cascading through her head. What follows is usually what one has feared. It becomes a self-fulfilling prophecy. When we hold beliefs that are positive in nature, our behavior becomes reflective of that more positive outlook. We are not born with a particular set of beliefs. We develop them through the course of time and experience. Our beliefs exert great power over our lives, be it positive or negative. Our very abilities are far from fixed. The same holds for our beliefs as well.

Exercise #3

The first step to cognitive interruption is write down all of the negative, rational self talk that you have experienced during periods of test anxiety. Take a moment to close your eyes, and recall your last test situation, what were your thoughts? What thoughts did you have at the beginning of the process? What did these thoughts develop into? The act of writing down the thoughts, no matter how irrational that that might seem, is helpful in that it makes them tangible and more real.

The next step is cognitive dispute. Take you to the negative and irrational thoughts and write a more reasonable, realistic dispute to them. This is also a step in what is known as "reality testing." If you have studied regularly and effectively, you know that you have prepared well for the exam. This fact allows you to dispute the thoughts like, "I didn't study hard enough" and "I'm going to fail." The disputes are reality testing that you develop become the basis for positive statements are affirmations. You will use these in the next step for conquering test anxiety. Affirmations are best kept brief. An example such as "I am well prepared" or "I know that I'm going to do well" are good examples of brief affirmations. Write your disputes as challenges to the negative thoughts, and his positive affirmations of your expected outcome.

Visualization is a performance-enhancing technique used by athletes all over the world. It involves creating a mental picture of a positive outcome. For example, a weightlifter, just prior to the lift will imagine seeing himself hoist the weight. His vision of the outcome will be an effortless lift. Many studies have demonstrated that weightlifters can lift far more poundage by visualizing the lift prior to executing it.

As a student, you want to create a mental image of a positive outcome around your taking a test. You may want to picture yourself calmly completing an exam. You may want to envision the return of the exam with a big red "A" on top of the test. The positive visual picture of a successful outcome is paired with positive affirmations that you created in the cognitive disputing step.

As you enter the exam room, as soon as you take your seat, begin the process of overcoming test anxiety. Start with the few repetitions of the quieting breathtaking. Continue with the brief progressive relaxation exercise. When you have eliminated the majority of your muscle tension start visualizing a positive outcome while you repeat in your mind, your positive affirmation. Through this phase, continue using the quieting breath technique. When the test arrives, take a quick quieting breath and just look the test over. This is a brief skimming of the test format and some of the questions. Determine a question or two that you readily know the answer to, or identify a section that looks particularly easy. You want to start the process with some immediate success. Answer these questions and complete that section of the test, then go back to the beginning and start sequentially running through the test. Use the quieting breath is needed to deal with any emerging anxiety.

Anxiety also plays a positive role in performance situations. It heightens your senses and if not excessive, can sharpen a recall of information. A certain amount of anxiety is an asset in any performance situation. It is important to remember that everyone experiences anxiety. It may not escalate to the full blown variety of test anxiety we have described here, but it precedes the taking of tests for every student.

Although low-level anxiety can be useful, lingering or chronic anxiety prior to the test is downright wearing. An excellent intervention tool is humor. Have on hand a collection of cartoons from a writer you like but don't read it until just before the test. Taking a humor break is a wonderful way to dissipate stress. What I like to call up "quick-burst humor," like that found in The Far Side, or Dilbert is particularly effective. Instead of cramming for an hour before the exam, he is time to take a humor break. This can be done alone or in a group. You will find that also adds some fun to the testing process. It can definitely improve your performance as well.

·11·

Guerrilla Study Techniques: Pareto's Efficiency Accomplished by Doing More in Less Time

Succes is not the result of spontaneous combustion. You must set yourself on fire.
-Reggie Leach

There are times when the tasks of school seem monumental. Balancing the workload of school against the demands of having to work or remain a part of your family can feel like it will swallow you and spit you out the other side. Long ago I was given the advice of not working harder, but working smarter. Of course that didn't give me the answers as to how I would go about doing that. Over the course of four degrees ranging from psychology to nursing, I refined several techniques that are the essence of "guerrilla study techniques." Just what are these study techniques? The name is taken from a specialized type of combat. Guerrilla soldiers function in small groups that are Rapid and highly mobile attack troops who often take on much larger foes. Guerrilla study techniques allow the student to cover a lot of ground very quickly, attacking a large workload with sufficient means and then moving on. This is Pareto's efficiency meeting the world of academia. These are ways of doing things that represent 20% of effort leading to 80% of results.

Churn and Burn Researching

In the beginning of the quarter, you will receive a course syllabus advising you of the assigned papers, their topic, and due dates. If you have from five to 10 papers to complete by the end of the quarter, with the requirement of five to 15 references for each, that could translate to a lot of library time.

The first question to ask yourself is, "Can any of these papers be related?" The answer is often yes. If this is the case, you can target one general subject area or topic and develop variations on the theme for each of the various papers. If you are taking a number of courses in your chosen field, you may even find that you can reuse variations of the same topic to different courses. This approach can consolidate both the number of references, you need and the required reading. There is no law that you must use a reference only once.

After you determine how to interrelate papers in a particular course or courses, take a look at the suggested reading for the course. Are there any summary articles in your reading list? Articles that are oriented to overviews of particular topics are a gold mine of references. They can also suggest an area you might develop into a paper. Read the overview article and use it to brainstorm related topics for your papers

Once you have figured out some tentative topics for your papers, turned to the reference section of the overview article. Here you will find a broad number of articles to help you in your research. Make a copy of the reference list and then highlight all of the articles it sound like promising references for your designated papers. Stick this in a folder and mark it "References-(course name)." Set it aside.

Reference lists are a tremendous resource if you're writing about a little researched subject. They can also raise a red flag on a topic which may cause you difficulty. For example, topic which has only one or two references listed may be just too narrow to provide you with enough material for the paper. You may want to rethink your choice of subject matter in a case where there is little written on a particular subject, look for reference lists for those articles you can find. As suggested, copy the reference lists and mark the ones that show promise. Stick them in the folder.

Next, make your initial scouting trip to the library (or if you can connect online with your school's library system, you can do this from home). The advantage of computer connectivity is that the system is open 24 hours a day, seven days a week. Perform your literature search by brainstorming possible keywords for your topic. Literature search engines, just like their Internet counterparts work from keywords. Many college libraries have classes on how to use the literature search engine, and I would recommend you take one. They are well worth your time. If your college or university has an "Informatics" department, they may have an introductory course in searching for information.

Plan on spending a block of time doing nothing but your literature search and gather all your references for all your papers in one sitting. Computer access would generally allow you to access the abstract for particular articles to assess the appropriateness for your papers. Your goal is to make the most efficient use of your time. Everything for one paper or course gets filed at the time it was gathered. Use your computer to cut and paste lists of references for each course. Highlight the ones with use in more than one so you don't gather them more than once.

The final fast-strike requires a partner. This can either be another student, friend or family member. You're going to divide and conquer the work of harvesting the reference literature. I suggest you and your partner attack this task on a low demand day for the library, usually the weekend. Buy an electronic copy card from the library for the copy machines, or if the library doesn't sell these, bring a roll of quarters. Your partner is going to do nothing but copy files and place them in folders.

Your job will be to search for specific articles so that you can come away with at least 90% of what you'll need to write your papers. We all have afterthoughts when we get into the middle of a project. Additional references can be obtained on an as-need basis. As you become more proficient with literature searching, you will have less and less need to obtain additional references. Highlighting everything from the same journal can copy all the pertinent articles at one time. If you gather all of the references from a particular journal at one time, you will stop making trips back and forth to the same place. Like the guerrilla soldier, you want to strike quickly and efficiently. You can complete the task in as little as one quarter of the time it would take you if you were to work on your own.

Remember to reciprocate your partner's help. If you are assisted by another student using the same strategy, you can return the favor. It becomes a mutually rewarding process. If a family member acted as your partner, find a way to show your appreciation. What your partner gave you is an extremely valuable commodity for a hard-working student -the gift of more time.

Condensed Reading

I often wondered if my professors truly believed that their course was the only thing I had going on in my life. The required reading at a college or graduate level may be the equivalent of reading War and Peace several times during the quarter. Some professional programs such as law and medicine make very high demands on the student's ability to read and absorb information. Sometimes it is impossible to keep up with the required reading. The reality is that you can't read every word. So how do you decide what and how you will read?

Start with the core reading for the class. This will be the most information-dense material. You will find that 80 to 90% of the material is an elaboration on concepts presented in the headings of the chapter. This material merits a more thorough reading them what you will do for the suggested or support literature. Your strategy is to read the first several paragraphs in a section. When the writer moves to material that clearly elaborates on the initial information in that section, move on to the next section.

The support readings are often not as content-dense is what you will likely find in the core reading. It will often be an expansion of aspects of the core content. This reading often is noted on a suggested list of readings given by an instructor. You may find them useful as references when you challenge the task of writing papers for your course. The instructor may give you a good source of references for papers in the suggested articles.

Research articles begin with an abstract which gives you a good overall sense of the contents of the article. After reading the abstract, move to the next section of the article, which will be a summary or an introduction to the problem. This section further defines the problem or issue discussed in the paper highlight key phrases in this section.

If the papers presented in an outline format, then each heading introduces the topic or main idea, which will be found in the lead sentence of the section. Quickly highlight the main idea of the section and move to the next session. This fast skimming allows you to quickly pull out the main ideas. Generally, the sections about subject populations and research methods can be paid only cursory attention or potentially skipped altogether. The abstract will often defined the subject population and the type of research tool used. If this is the case, highlight them in the abstract, and skip the sections altogether.

The summary or conclusions section merits full reading. This is the essence of what the researcher has found. The organization of this section can be distilled into an outline format. Look for sentences that make statements. That is where you will find what the investigators believed to be fact based on their research.

Narrative papers follow the same organization that you will. When you write a term paper or respond to an essay question. The starting point is an overview of the problem. Highlight the key points and be able to summarize the problem, premise, or issue discussed in the paper. The first subject heading is a clear demarcation of the end of the initial summary of the paper's content. From that point on the paper can be viewed as an outline, with section headings, forming the markers for new ideas and content.

Each subject heading can be broken down further. The lead sentence states the idea of a paragraph. Here's where the student picks up speed, underline the idea or concept for a section and then move on. If a section or beginning of a paragraph grabs your interest or seems to have more content in it, by all means, read it all. Keep in mind, your goal is to rapidly move through the meat of the paper to the summary or conclusions section.

In a distraction-free environment, each paper can be reviewed in a range of two to 10 minutes. Retention of the material is increased by transferring the information to 5 x 7 inch card which will be used in other guerrilla techniques. Start by writing the reference at the top of the card. This should follow the approved APA reference style as it is exactly the same way you will format the reference in your bibliography.

Next write down what the paper found or concluded. Include the name of the population studied. This should be a brief statement. Here is an example:

"Correctional officers have shortened lifespan due to occupational stress."

Return to the subsections of the paper defined the factors which support the conclusion. Using the same example, we would list the factors underneath our initial statement that comes directly from the subject headings in the paper.

"Correctional officers have shortened lifespan due to occupational stress." Pg. 24

- low decision-making autonomy with high-level responsibility.
- physically and mentally hostile environment; assault/hostage potential. Pg. 26
- little opportunity for advancement. Pg. 27
- rigid schedules/shift work; little accommodation for needs a family. Pg. 31
- mandatory overtime/ little choice about working many hours in a week. Pg. 32
- isolation from coworkers. Pg. 33

Other reverse side of the card, note any sentences that are particularly striking. If it makes a point well, or a conclusion in a clear and compelling manner, it can be used later as a quote in the paper, or in class discussion.

Writing cards out in this manner will help you in a number of different ways. Your retention of information is going to be minimal, if all you do is scan the material. Creating a card allows you to better imprint the material in your memory as well as integrated with other information. The cards can be quickly reviewed, creating repetitions of the information. These cards will also come into play in two other guerrilla techniques.

Class Expert

An academic course can be looked upon as an explicit contract between student and instructor. Both agreed to perform their responsibilities to create a successful educational experience.

The instructor brings expertise in a prepared presentation to class. They create the opportunity for that students will learn. The student comes to class with assignments completed in prepared to be an active participant in the class. In many courses, discussion makes up a significant part of the time spent in the classroom, and can comprise a large part of the overall evaluation of the student. When you come to a class hungry for information and ready to actively participate in discussion and the experience is far more satisfying for the instructor. Often they will put more into their presentation when they know they selection of students who are active and articulate in the discussion.

Bringing your participation to a higher level builds on the previous guerrilla technique of translating your reading to cards. The "class expert" is really the one who displays the most expertise with the material. You can achieve this by simply having the relevant cards at your fingertips during class discussion. It allows you to reference specific content from your reading. You can also add additional points to your reference cards as they come out in class discussion.

Think about the message you're sending to an instructor. When you can reference specific information from suggested or ancillary reading, you make a strong statement that you are a student who is committed to a higher level of understanding. You demonstrate your effort and academic capability and distinguish yourself from other students a tangible way. In the competitive world of academics, you rise above the herd.

The payoffs from this level of participation are many. First and foremost is your own learning. Actively engaging in thought and discussion of material seats this in your memory. The recall is far more potent when you have experienced this level of integration from active discussion. Good grades become a natural conse-quence of putting your learning first.

Opportunity goes to those were perceived as most diligent and capable. When you prepare yourself as I have suggested, you demonstrate that you possess both of these attributes. Instructors are often very aware of the opportunities that may not be open to everyone. They can open doors for you that otherwise would be closed if you are viewed as simply an average student.

Just think how much more powerful a letter of recommendation can be from an instructor, whom you have impressed with your preparation and hunger for education. When you have established this kind of relationship with your teachers, they may prove to be an invaluable asset for future networking. They can write a more personal letter of recommendation and they may steer opportunities your way.

The One-Sitting Paper

The topic of your paper has been decided. References have been collected and evaluated. An outline of the main argument of your paper and the factors which support your conclusions have been completed. You are about raid to get started with the actual writing.

Even though you may have all your reference materials at hand, you will find putting your finger on the right piece of information that you need to be difficult. More than likely you have lots of papers with information. Shuffling through information to find one particular fact is a waste of time. The more you look for more disorganize your pile of papers becomes soon any semblance of organization can be lost as you search in vain to find the critical facts. You know are out there somewhere.

Most of us have been down this trail before. Not only is it frustrating, but it is time-consuming and inefficient and it interrupts the writing process, making it difficult to keep up with the flow of writing a paper. This is another instance where you can use guerrilla techniques to work smarter instead of harder.

Take your outline in the card you made when you were gathering your reference materials quickly read through the cards. In a corner, label them either with letters or numbers. Return to your outline, and reference which card the information which supports that portion of the paper. Once this is completed, tape up your outline, so you can readily referred to it.

Clear off your desk and in place all of the cards in the workspace around you they can be organized based on how you will use them in the course of the paper. Just as it is true about the articles you have read, 80 to 90% of the paper's content will support and embellish a particular point or issue in the body of the paper.

The substance of the expansion of your outline comes directly from the reference material. With your cards you have all the information right at your fingertips. You have made note of the article and page number where a particular piece of information is found. As you move through your paper, you have the specific reference and the page number right on your card. Bada-boom, bada-bing! You're back to writing right away. You have eliminated the distraction of hunting desperately for pieces of information. You are able to maintain your momentum and train of thought.

For every paper you write, you must list references cited in that paper. This can be a tedious task, if you have to go back to copies of the original material and creates citations in the correct format making your reference cards as I have suggested allows you to have that at your fingertips, in the correct format. All you need to do is arrange your resources in alphabetical order and copy what you previously written. You have illuminated the need to search and shuffle through piles of paper, and create references in the appropriate format.

An alternative for doing a bibliography that saves typing and lots of work is to use the copy and paste and split screen features on your computer. Some articles are published in their entirety. Copy and paste the reference section to a master bibliography file. The right click split screen feature on PC style computers can place both the article and your master list on the same screen. Cull any references that are not on your list either at the beginning when you first copy a reference list or when you have completed copying to the mast reference file. When you are adding the bibliography to your paper, use the spit screen again. Copy and paste from the master reference file. These references are already going to be in APA format. Highlight the list and change the font and print style to match what you have in your paper. You have spared yourself the tedium and need for attention to fine detailed work. People with ADD/ADHD brains generally find this a time when their mind is prone to wander.

When you finish your last reference, you can throw up your hands because you're pretty much done. Don't forget to use spell check and grammar check. Print a hard copy and set it aside. Often times having a cool off after you write a paper allows you to come back and do the final polishing with a fresh set of eyes. Writing a successful paper comes from following a series of well thought out steps. Putting the words down on paper develops a flow. What maintains the flow is keeping distractions to a minimum. With the methods I have described, you minimize internal distractions and can cut down your writing time by as much as half. Again you are becoming a guerrilla student: lightning fast and ruthlessly efficient in completing your tasks, and moving on.

Word Recognition Software

I am a fairly inept typist. On a good day, I can do 30 words per minute. That doesn't include the time, where I will go back and correct mistakes. I also am a fairly terrible speller. I have always been thankful for tools found on the computer that allow me to check my spelling. They are far from perfect, but the unfortunate truth is they still better than I do. This book was written with word recognition software. These programs are not perfect. Their accuracy ranges from 90 to 100%. Sometimes you get some interesting and humorous misreads. It makes a thorough review reading of your material an absolute. They will accept language at an excess of 100 words per minute.

Various things affect their accuracy. You'll program them to your voice. If you have a cold, the accuracy will diminish. It is important to be a quiet space. External noise can lead to misinterpretations of your words. If you cough or sneeze, generally the filter will not register the sounds because it will exceed the volume limit.

The real advantage to these is creating flow. Often times it is easy to write a paper with this method because it feels like we are just talking to another person, explaining information in our conclusions. We tend to speak in a natural way, which allows us to not have sentences that are way too long. If it does not sound right to the ear, likely it's awkward when it's in print. There is also the advantage of being able to look at the screen as it translates your words to print. You can quickly see your misreads, and go back and correct them without ever having to touch the keyboard. I use this technology in my private practice. I can dictate therapy notes which are far more complete and detailed. There is a far greater ease in doing it this way, as opposed to typing my notes. It is a profound timesaver. You may have developed the ability to type with a high degree of proficiency. If you have learned to do this, that's great, and more power to you. If you are a marginal typist like me, this is technology well worth considering. It is also not overly expensive.

Guerrilla Study Groups

Guerrilla study groups have a number of factors in common with the guerrilla fighting unit. Both guerrilla soldiers and guerrilla students are bound together by a common goal. Common goals create a powerful degree of motivation supported and reinforced by the group's members. The smallness of the group be they soldiers or students is what makes the unit, highly efficient. There is a minimum of waiting for group members to catch up on moving quickly through enemy territory or study material. Tasks can be divided among members, all aimed at common good.

The advantage for the ADD/ADHD college student is that groups study inherently utilizes multiple representational systems at once (auditory, visual, and kinesthetic with social anchoring) to enhance learning. The more representational system we can employ, the better the recall and seating information into long term memory.

Group learning is a synergistic process. We all have our own thoughts about material to be studied. The impact of an issue is different on all of us given our varying life experiences. We think in similar yet unique ways. The advantage of group study is that we can gain perspectives and insights beyond our own.

Several factors surround the group process and increase motivation. Just like a row of soldiers fighting for a single cause, a group study binds students to a shared task. These mutual goals increase the degree of affiliation and investment of group members. It will evoke a higher level of expectation about the performance of individual members. This internal dynamic serves to make each individual feel more responsible for not letting the group down as a whole. This motivational synergy is extraordinarily powerful. It creates an accountability that might not exist when a student studies alone.

Group study moves a student beyond learning through passive reception of information. Like the example for medical education of "see one, do one, teach one," group study involves that final step -teaching. This presses the individual to attain a higher level of understanding of the material. If you want to understand a certain field of study, learn it so well that you can teach it to others. A higher degree of understanding of the material will result integration and clarity evolves from the challenge of having to explain concepts to other people. The division of labor in guerrilla study groups places each individual member in a position of teaching a specific area he or she has researched to others within the group.

I have found that the most effective groups are limited to three or four people. More members can complicate the process and reduce the efficiency of the group. When you study in common areas, classmates may see you ask to join the group. You may find it difficult to say no. Because of the focus, task-directed nature of the group, study group membership must be fixed. To avoid this kind of problem, find a space free of distraction of having foot traffic walking by you. It will save you the task of setting limits on casual membership to the group.

How do you select group members? Do you want people who will lead to the energy and effort of a group? It helps to be a bit of a detective when looking for good study habits. For example, in a class, take note of who is consistently on time. This small factor is often a reflection of the persons work habits and attitudes toward their education. Look for the person sits in the class. Unless the instructor has assigned specific seats, where the person chooses to sit is very revealing. There is a direct correlation between the persons grades and the proximity to the front of the classroom. The top students tend to sit near the front. They strive to get every bit of information they can out of class. More active participation in group discussion is going to come largely from the front half of the class. Less able or less confident students are more likely to be found in the back of the room, where they can be passive rather than active participants.

When you ask people if they would like to form a study group, be sure that you discuss the format and expectations for group members. Sharing the information from this chapter can be a good starting point. The group is going to be common entity. Rules and norms for the group will quickly develop. Members must understand and be committed to the process of the group from the beginning if your group is going to be highly focused and goal directed. A crucial question for members to answer is whether they can commit to a study group with an active plan for continued study. The answer must be "yes" for all members, or the group will be less likely to accomplish its goal.

Once the group members are established, discussions can now turn to how to structure study time. There are many different ways to study. A group may want to use repetition and drill. This is a useful strategy when faced with the task of command of a high volume of facts. The class material may lend itself more to group discussion. Courses of study like law often stress integration of material in addition to recall of facts. You do not have to stick with one format. It is likely that you will develop a hybrid of several methods of review.

The efficiency of a force of guerrilla soldiers comes from their ability to share responsibilities while developing an expertise in a specialized area. You want members of your study group to function like this as well. You accomplish this by assigning duties to each member of the group. Divide up the material to be covered for each week and determine who will be running each meeting. Make sure this is done on a rotating basis. As the leader, each member will have the opportunity to step into the role of teacher.

In the week prior to your turn as study group leader, you'll have more preparation for the meeting than usual. The good news is that you have to do this only one quarter or a fifth of the time. You can prepare by writing down potential study questions as you go through your reading. Do this by asking yourself "If I were the teacher, what would I ask my students to test their knowledge?" As you come up with relevant questions, you spontaneously start to think about how you would answer them. When you move into the role of teacher it forces you to attain a higher level of integration. You must push yourself to take the important step beyond just absorbing the information. You will find that the material you present in the group will be the material you have the best recall on when you are tested.

A few days prior to the exam, the group should run a review session that encompasses all of the information. Resist the temptation to do this before just the test. Each person runs part of the total review, taking the part he or she was responsible for. This session requires no additional work. It is a review of what you have already covered. After the reviews completed the members moved to individual study using whatever means works best for them.

If schedules can be coordinated to squeeze in a short review the day of the exam you'll take on a different format. Each member is encouraged to bring up one or two areas for final clarification keeping discussion brief and specific. This is not a time for repetition and drill. This only creates pressure and increases stress.

I find a good way to cap off pre-test jitters at the meeting is to use humor to defuse tension. During one of my pretest review sessions in graduate school group of us would share books of various cartoonists or other humorous writing. This gave us all a much needed laugh. Laughter has an amazing power to relax both the mind and body. You know the material at this point, if you don't, it's too late anyway. Some of the material, you probably know so well you could even get in front of the class and teach it. It's time to let go. Its time to clear out the brain and get loosened up for the test.

The need to debrief after a difficult challenge is a natural way to relieve stress. Coming out of class, the first thing people ask each other is how they did on the test and what answers were of a particular question to them. Your study group may or may not want to debrief is a group after the exam. Decided this before you take the test. If you are going to get together, make it a time to let down, to offer support and encouragement to other group members. The last thing you want to do is extend your anxiety about the test.

If you decide to let down after a test on your own, know what will help you decompress most effectively. You might find exercise is a good relax and. Maybe you need to just "veg out" in front of the TV. Decompression is an important component to dynamic study. You have to wind down before you can move on to the next challenge. Take some time to discover what works best for you.

Power Presentations

The number one fear most people admit to have is the fear of public speaking. Second place goes to the fear of dying. Comedian Jerry Seinfeld pointed out that if you're at a funeral, this means you'd rather be the person in the box than the one giving the eulogy.

Giving presentations is an unavoidable requirement of most educational programs. For many people, the prospect of standing up in front of peers and professionals alike provokes extreme anxiety. The fight-flight response will kick in. Mostly it's about flight! Your mouth goes dry. Your voice quavers. Your heart begins to race. You're overcome with an overwhelming urge to go to the bathroom, as you wonder how you will ever get to the presentation. Rest assured, even the best speakers have experienced high anxiety when giving talks.

A starting point for giving effective presentations is gaining control over your anxiety. In talking about test anxiety in the previous sections of this book, I gave several exercises for controlling the physiological response to anxiety. The quieting breath is a highly useful exercise for doing quickly with an anxious state. Insert a notation in your presentation telling yourself to pause and take a breath. This is not only a useful way to control anxiety, but a great way to pace your presentation.

I remember my first paid, professional presentation. I was to give a 15 minute talk to a group of parents from a Head Start program. I had prepared what I considered to be about 40 minutes of presentation, leaving the remainder for questions and answers. My anxiety level was so high that I raced through my material finishing in about 15 minutes. I had a moment of utter horror when I realized that I had another 30 minutes to fill. Thinking quickly, I divided the parents into small groups for discussion of hastily devised questions. While I pulled it off in a successful way, I vowed never to repeat this experience again. This didn't mean I was giving up on public speaking. I've gone on to conduct workshops with audiences of over 250 people. It did mean that I needed to learn some things about presentations.

The most effective presentations use all of the sensory reception modalities. You want people to look, listen and feel. The most successful speakers understand that the average attention span for an audience is only about 10 minutes. The drier the material is shorter the attention span. If the speaker is particularly engaging or the subject is of particular interest, a listener may be able to focus for as long as 15 minutes before losing concentration. This applies to people without ADD/ADHD.

Attention span also dictates how much content you can share. If you had 50 minutes to fill, plan on presenting no more than five major points or pieces of information. Just as in written work, 80 to 90% of the speeches embellishment of the main points of the presentation. More technical presentations may make five to seven main points. Be aware that too much core content can overwhelm an audience. Your presentation will be seen as more effective if you present fewer ideas and then effectively expand on them.

State what you want the student to come away with knowing. Asking the audience a question is a good way to get an attention break. Having them write down their most relevant experience or memory is another way of creating an attention shift and gaining another ten minute interval of attention.

Another way to increase attention span is by switching between receptor pathways. The most effective presentations get people up and moving at regular intervals. Elementary education teachers are perhaps the most aware of us need to move. Nowhere are the limits on attention more noticeable than with children. The effective teacher finds a way to let students stand, stretch and move around. Even though our attention span increases as we get older, we need to move around or have an attention shift or we lose our focus.

Clearly, some of the most effective and charismatic speakers can be found on televised religious programs. They are masters to playing to all of the receptor pathways. They vary the cadence of their voice. They use lavish backdrops. They interrupted talks with a song from the choir that is vibrantly alive in both auditory and visual components. They demand people get up and move.

Spend some time watching a few of these programs for their presentation style. They can teach you a great deal about the dynamics of public speaking. Many motivational speakers use the very same techniques. People leave, not only with useful information, they also feel charged up and excited. Although you may not need to have your audience feel energized in this way, you do want to hold their attention.

Verbal Presentation

The most difficult task for new speaker is how to evenly pace the presentation. The mistake I shared in rushing through my presentation is very common. New speakers have a tendency to speed up when they talk because there is such a hurry to get it over with. Here are a few pointers to keep you falling into that trap. Preparing your notes properly can help you slow down your presentation. Notes should not be used to tell you exactly what to say. They are only reminders of what you need to talk about regarding your content. You don't want to read your presentation.

There are two exceptions to this rule. The beginning sentence for your talk, and the use of exact quotes are the only times you should be reading. Reading the first sentence particularly if it has a thought provoking 'hook' allows you to pace and have a moment to quell any performance anxiety. I will use a quieting breath after my first sentence. It slows me down and adds drama by allowing the starting statement to sink in.

The idea of using a 'hook' statement or question to draw your audience in is best illustrated in popular fiction. The first line or at best paragraph must entice the reader to want to go further. In my opinion, one of the best writers for 'first line hooks' is Dean Koontz. For example, take the opening line for his book Velocity (Bantam Books, June 2005):

"With a draft beer and a smile, Ned Pearsall raised a toast to his deceased neighbor, Henry Friddle, whose death greatly pleased him."

How can you not be drawn in by that hook? Opening statements to the best talks do the same thing. The evoke curiosity and provoke questioning. Return to the section on structuring a paper and you have the variety of formats for public speaking. The additional layer is pacing, having attention breaks at roughly ten minute intervals. You can use multiple hooks during a talk. The very best speakers naturally do this. A fun exercise that builds awareness of the hook is to go the book rack for best-selling novels and just read the first paragraph of each book. Time to use your creativity in crafting your own hook to your speaking

Start by writing down a salutation of first sentence of your presentation. I put this in bold block letters at least half an inch high. You want to be able to see your notes by just glancing down at them. At the end of the first spoken line, write. "Pause!" The purpose of this cause is twofold. Did you time to compose yourself and relax. It provides a perfect interval for taking a quieting breath. It also gives your audience time to absorb what you have said.It's then time to roll out the hook. Write this down as well.

The next part of your presentation notes should contain different pieces of information to support your main point. These are brief, as you should be familiar enough with your subject of the short reminders all you need to launch into talking about your subject. You should have reminders for each ten minute section of a presentation. I'll often write down a joke that I tie into a particular point of content. Humor is a powerful way to deliver content.

We spend a good portion of our day talking with others. When we give a presentation, our anxiety erases the idea that the essence of what we are doing is talking with people. If we view our speech as directing conversation, we can certainly eliminate some of our apprehension. There are a number of techniques speakers can use to overcome audience intimidation. Some speakers picture are audiences wearing funny glasses and those who were wearing only their underwear.

A very helpful technique is making eye contact with members of the audience. At first, you might think this would be distracting to you as a speaker. Instead, it actually keeps you moving along at an easy, steady pace. Think of it is similar to what you do when you're driving. You often checked the rearview and side mirrors or glanced your left or right. Your attention is not diverted. You have a better idea of the kinds and conditions you're driving in because of brief scanning.

As you learn to incorporate making eye contact in your presentations, you may want to try putting a colored mark at regular intervals in your presentation notes. This can provide a visual cue to cause, take a breath, or make eye contact. I generally make five to 10 eye contacts per minute during a presentation. I don't spend very long looking at one person. In large groups, the duration of an eye scan lengthens since, as you want to make sure eye contact is established. Using this technique, you can get members of a larger audience the feeling that your presentation is quite personal. Nothing makes a speech seemed more wooden than a speaker who does not make eye contact with the audience.

Practice your timing by watching and listening to yourself in front of a mirror. Saying the words out loud, tells you whether your initial sentence is clear and understandable. If the sentence is awkward or doesn't readily flow, you want to fix it now. When you're in front of an audience, it will be too late.

How do you look when you're giving your presentation? Are you fixed or rigid? Do nervously fidget with your hands? 90% of communication is nonverbal. Which her body expresses is extremely important. Spend some time observing people in ordinary conversation. You will notice that they are constantly moving. Many people not only move their head, but also their hands, arms, shoulders, even bodies when they are talking.

What movements to make when you're speaking? As you repeatedly practice your presentation, start incorporating eye scan and hand movements. You will make giving to your presentation easier for your audience, and yourself.

What allows a comedian to get the right timing, so the presentation is funny? The answer is practice, -lots and lots of practice. You need to do the same thing if you're going to be fresh, interesting, and worth listening to.

Visual Presentation

In addition to your own visual presentation, some speakers will use handouts to create visual interest. Depending on content, sometimes this can be a distraction to an audience. I will often announced to an audience that they do not need to take notes, and that everything is contained in the materials they have been given. When people transfer their attention to a handout, they take it away from you. Slides, computer-generated programs of graphics, even videos can be useful in adding positive visual dimension to your presentation. Use of these dimensions of visual presentation keeps the audience focus in your direction. The shifts to projected graphics, or video clips can shift attention just enough to sustain attention longer.

Physical Pathways

Have you ever notice what happens during a long class when an instructor goes past the usual break time? People start shifting in their chairs. They look up at the clock. They start to whisper among themselves. In short, they lose their ability to pay attention. Whenever possible, you want to get people moving at some point during the course of the presentation. If you can't reasonably get people to stand up and move, have them handle things. Years ago, I was in a lecture in sensory changes with advanced age. The presenter handed out cheap sunglasses smeared with Vaseline, which we were instructed to put on. He had this tape pieces of cotton to her fingertips of them put rubber gloves on our hands. We stuffed our ears with cotton balls. The presenter then asked us to do simple activities like picking up coins, reading normal sized print, and having a conversation. This exercise communicated more about the sensory changes in the elderly than any amount of talking with accomplished. We learned on an experiential level. The learning was powerful and long lasting. It also broke up the presentation by interjecting something other than verbal information. The element of fun lightened what could've been a very dry subject.

Inserting a physical element into the presentation is a challenge to your creativity. It can be an immensely powerful addition. A presentation that makes a few points effectively will be better received than one that covers more information, but loses the audience in the process.

Effective presentations require a variety of skills. Realize that you aren't going to acquire these overnight. As with any skill, it requires practice and what athletes call game day experience. Good speakers are not born, they develop through time.

·12·
Motivation

A preoccupation with the future not only prevents
us from seeing the present as it is but often
prompts us to rearrange the past.
-Eric Hoffer

Passion makes the world go round. Love makes it
a safer place.
-Ice T

You have a vision for yourself and your future. If you enter the academic vortex, riding shotgun is an established life filled with commitments to family and a career. You have placed yourself in a situation where your inner resources will be rigorously tested whether your course through school lasts one year or ten. You still need to sustain yourself economically, physically, emotionally, and spiritually. The demands of your life will not go away.

You may ask yourself, "How my going to do all of this?" In using this book, you will learn a number of skills and techniques for helping you succeed in managing all of the demands of school place on you. Is this right for me? A reasonable question, as you wonder if you can continue to juggle all the balls that you have in the air.

This may be another return to school. Several clients I work with have started and stopped college several times after struggling to keep up. Many of these had the message from parents that they would not continue to receive financial support with such poor performance. Any aspect of fun or enjoyment in the process of education had ceased under the burden of a message of failure. Every time they dropped out of an academic program felt like a failure on a number of levels. Every re-entry was questioned. Will this be the time I complete my degree? Will I finally succeed? Academic struggle and ADD/ADHD are not synonymous but they are frequent bed fellows.

What do you need and value in your life? What fuels and sustains you as an individual? A premise that I held in my own process of education was that if I lost what was most important to me, I had not succeeded. It didn't matter what letters I had attached to my name, or what job I could acquire as a result of my training because it would have been a hollow victory, if I didn't have the people who are important to me still in my life.

Sometimes people question the very nature of going to school, in light of the important people in their life. I have had clients that have been stuck in indecision right up to the 11th hour of leaving the area to go to school. They worried about the impact that their decision would have on their family. Ambivalence is a swamp they can keep people stuck for a long time. Ignoring your aspirations has its own cost. Some of the most difficult regrets we have in our life revolve around things we wanted to do, but for some reason did not.

As a therapist, it is my job to help guide people out of the swamp of ambivalence. I want to help them challenge their beliefs, and the behaviors that grow from those beliefs. Sometimes the best way to get a grasp on the problem, is to view all of the facets of a problem at once. I will have people do a cost/benefit analysis. This is a fairly easy process. It can be adapted to any problem, where somebody finds themselves stuck in making a decision.

Exercise: Examining the Risk

Step 1: This is basically forming what is called a decision square. If you make a choice, or you elect to stay where you are, both are decisions. Not making a decision, is a de facto way of selecting an outcome. I suggest that you take a piece of paper, and folded into four quadrants. Each section will have its own question. It should look something like this:

What is the best outcome/ best thing that can happen by choosing to make this decision?

What is the worst outcome/ worst thing that can happen by choosing to make this decision?

What is the best outcome/ best thing that can happen if I choose to remain where I am?

What is the worst outcome/ worst thing that can happen if I choose to remain where I am?

Step 2: The next step is to create each of the different factors found in each quadrant. Give them a numerical score based on what you value in your life. Often times the right decision will have emerged before you give things a rating. Given how our brains are wired, seeing the big picture brings clarity. Some other questions remain.

Step 3: This step is about pragmatics. Ask yourself the question, who will be most affected by your decision? A significant other, and certainly children need to be considered in this. A "worst outcome" in my own consideration of going to school was the risk of growing up, distant and unavailable for my child. The irony involved was that much of my motivation and going to school was about being able to provide a better life for my family. This question can be answered by plugging it back in to the decision square.

Step 4: The process of change is intertwined with taking some risk. We can go through life without taking any risks. While we can insulate ourselves from disappointment, physical and emotional pain, we've lost the opportunity for greater joy, satisfaction, and often the essence of what makes life worth living. It is important to ask yourself why are you doing this. Any decision involving some risk is best examined in the light of questioning what your motives and your values are.

Values and Rewards

We are guided by our values. Whether you're in touch with them or not, you have values. Often times we only figure out what a value is when one has been breached. They are beacons which underscore our beliefs, expectations and preferences. Our values are a powerful motivational tool. It helps to understand what our values are and clarify their meaning in our lives. Success is ultimately dependent on living your life in a way that is congruent and consistent with your values.

The other factor that motivates us is found in the nature of reward. Rewards are about what we want for ourselves. It is really important that we reward ourselves. I have an assignment that I give to all of my clients to do when they complete the other assignments given to them. This comes right from something called "social learning theory." The thumbnail explanation is that the world, at large, is very poor at telling us that we did a good job. Research tells us that the very worst jobs are ones where people receive no feedback. Running a close second are jobs where only negative feedback is offered. When we depend on the external world to tell us were doing a good job, it is quite likely that we'll be disappointed.

When a client completes an assignment, they have to perform what I call a Mandatory Part 'B' Assignment. They need to find some positive, self nurturing way of rewarding in themselves. This is preceded by mentally connecting the dots, and reflecting why they are doing a positive behavior for themselves. When we go to work, things are very straightforward. We work so many hours, our employer pays us so many dollars. It is like Pavlov's dog. When the bell rings, a food pellet drops. Pretty soon the dog salivates just hearing the bell. I want to develop an internal environment where people can acknowledge themselves as having done a good job.

Rewards can also encompass the important people in our lives. It may be justifying taking some time off to go to dinner and a movie with your significant other. Mutual playtime sustains relationships. It works that way for both adults and for children, if you have them. Like a plant without water, our relationships will suffer if they don't continue to be nourished. That nourishment can serve as our own reward.

We know from brain research that the most powerful receptor pathway is visual. When I was going to school and burning the candle at both ends with full-time work, and full-time education, I was very clear about what I wanted for my own reward. This happened to be a boat. Alongside the pictures of my family that were posted where I could readily see them on my desk, I placed a brochure from the boat that I wanted. This provided a visual reminder for an outcome I hope to achieve at the end of the process.

There was an episode of "The Simpsons," where Homer

realized he was in an unsatisfying job, and he asked himself the fundamental question of, "Why am I doing this?" He then inadvertently found a picture of his daughter, Maggie. The answer to that question became clear in an instant as he placed her picture on his desk. Ask yourself the question of who is most important in your life. Also ask yourself whether what you want for yourself is uniquely for you as a result of your efforts. It's time to add those visual reminders of who is important to, and what you want for yourself to your field of vision.

Dare to Push the Growing Edge

For the person who has grown up with ADD/ADHD, particularly if it has been untreated, a variety of beliefs may stem from this experience. You may think back to your own experience. Did you ever have a teacher or parent, say you were lazy or stupid? Sometime the message is unspoken but it is just as clear. Did you have trouble recalling information during tests, or in front of a class? Did you have trouble meeting deadlines, and search for excuses as to why you didn't have your homework, yet another time? These and other negative messages form a foundation for negative beliefs. Something that may cut you off from getting the assistance to do your very best is an independent style of doing things. Deadlines can be the great motivator for the ADD person and lends to a heroic individual effort done on your own.

An important realization for people who have not had treatment for their ADD/ADHD is that a significant barrier to their success has been reduced or removed. Assumptions about one's abilities were based on a period of struggle. It wasn't a choice to struggle, but an outcome of a normal difference in brain functioning. This same brain difference can be the very factor which can propel them to success that previously was felt to be out of their reach. Moving into a new learning style and method can represent a big change. The Examining the Risk exercise can help you challenge some of your previous notions about how to go about the tasks of school and challenge beliefs.

The power of getting help and assisting people in challenging their beliefs is the really fun part of treating people with ADD/ADHD. I share this story of one of my clients who is pushing the growing edge of his beliefs. It is also an example of the adage that success has many mothers.

Rob's Story

Rob is a man in his 30s that came to me on a referral from his therapist. He was in recovery from full blown alcohol dependence. He had a bachelor's degree, but was working at a job, far below his educational level. Substance abuse disorders are quite common for people with ADD/ADHD, as is an erratic job history, and not working up to a level commensurate with their education. His therapist recognized that there were issues beyond his recovery, and that likely he had ADD/ADHD.

When I explored Rob's history, I found that he had been to quite a number of different colleges, and it'd taken him almost 8 years to obtain his bachelor's degree. His degree was in "General Studies." He had enough credits to graduate, but not enough in any one subject to define a major so it was packaged as a generalist degree. This demonstrated he had the persistence to make it to the point where a degree was granted. School had been an enormous struggle. Rob had problems with deadlines. He did not test well. He had all of the struggles that one associates with untreated ADD/ADHD.

When Rob is formally tested, he clearly had profound symptoms for inattention. He had less pronounced symptoms for hyperactivity. I started him on a course of stimulant medications. He had a wonderful response. I'll never forget our first follow-up session after he started on medications. He shared with me, the fact that he had read a book cover-to-cover. He stated that he had never done this before in his life. He also shared that he had read the book in two sessions. He had tears in his eyes as he explained he never knew how things could be so different, and he could actually get things done. He took me by surprise as the session ended, by giving me a bear hug, and telling me he felt that would majorly changed his life.

Several changes evolved for Rob. His sobriety grew far more comfortable. He was eventually able to let go of frequent AA meetings as a support. He worked with the therapist for a while longer, and then felt he was ready to call an end to therapy.

He added the number of behavioral prescriptions that I had suggested for him. He began daily aerobic exercise, and over several months and dropped 40 pounds. He started reading about organizational skills, and adopting the practices he found in these resources.

Rob had always dreamed of going to law school. He never believed that this was at all possible. He decided to challenge this belief and entered a study course for the LSAT. When he took this test, he turned in a solid set of scores. He was allowed a couple of accommodations, which we applied for prior to his taking the test. At the time of this printing, Rob is in the process of applying to law schools. He has talked to some of the local schools, and his previous sub-par academic performance is not likely to be a factor that will keep him out of law school. This was accomplished by naming his difficulties in his personal statement. I fully believe that he will get into law school. He will bring both passion and compassion to the profession.

Not everyone's course follows a path of such struggle. In the bell shaped curve of intelligence, people with ADD/ADHD often have high intelligence. Psychiatrist Howard Gardner developed the theory that there are different kinds of intelligence (1). Conventional IQ testing only evaluates logical and linguistic intelligence. Gardner names seven different types of intelligence. They consist of the following:

- *Musical Intelligence*
- *Bodily-Kinesthetic Intelligence*
- *Logical-Mathematical Intelligence*
- *Linguistic Intelligence*
- *Spatial Intelligence*
- *Interpersonal Intelligence*
- *Intrapersonal Intelligence*
- *Naturalistic Intelligence*

I find that many people in my practice really excel in various types of intelligence, sometimes dramatically so. The ability to think synthesizing multiple factors at once seems to be a strong trend for people with ADD/ADHD. The median educational level for my practice is something above a Masters degree. I have a number of clients who work in the trades, and who are not college-educated.

Some people with ADD/ADHD only experience struggles when the academic bar is raised quite high. For a psychologist that I see, it was always in the top 10% of his academic class. When he went to graduate school, he found himself in the bottom third of the class. This was a position that he never imagined he would be in. He reflected that being in the bottom third of his class was humiliating. He is truly a master therapist who has very high levels of interpersonal and intrapersonal intelligence. He has found a significant benefit in his practice with treatment for his ADD/ADHD. He can now sustain attention to work his way through complicated forensic assessments. His professional life is easier as a result of having focus.

Affirmations

The difficulty in turning around negative thoughts lies in the fact that over time we become very good at developing an internal critic. It arises out of our unconscious. It can lead to discounting the positives that we do receive. Have you ever had difficulty accepting a compliment? Our internal self has ways of devaluing complements. We tell ourselves, "Oh, he was just saying that," or "She probably says that to everyone." Think back to a compliment that you discounted. Was that a person in sincere in their comment? Was he or she indeed, "just saying that?" Of course not. They gave you positive feedback because they meant it.

A technique often used in group psychotherapy with the press people is "the compliment circle." It illustrates and helps people reality-test the negative critic that lies within. Group members take turns writing down something positive. They have experienced with another group member. It is read before the group, direct it at a particular participant. The receiver of a complement to give one of three responses:

1. *Thank you.*
2. *I like hearing that.*
3. *Say that again.*

Members explore whether they thought the compliment was insincere. Those receiving the compliment then ask the person giving the compliment, if they meant what they said. You can guess the outcome of this. If you feel uncomfortable when you get a positive comment, then your internal critic is alive and well, working to diminish positive feelings about yourself.

Affirmations are positive statements that we make about ourselves, about ourselves. They reflect beliefs. It's true we may not feel as though we have accepted the belief when we start out saying an affirmation. It does however give us a focus from which that change in behavior can emerge. As we experience a change in our behavior, the belief becomes internalized.

When my son was a toddler, I experienced a lot of frustration in my parenting. I struggled with my lack of patience. I was dealing with normal two-year-old behaviors. The use of affirmations gave me a focus that led me to both reflect on, and correct the behaviors which I was dissatisfied with. Affirming to myself that "I can be more patient" allowed me to step back from situations, and stop acting so impatiently and abrupt myself. I would carry this thought for the day with me, reflecting upon it as needed. It quelled the internal critic that negated when I was doing well. It also pointed out where I could do better as a parent.

Let me warn you right now, when you first start working with affirmations, they're going to sound dumb. You might find them silly or embarrassing. They may strike you as stilted and artificial. What's interesting is that we don't feel the same way when we beat ourselves up with negative affirmations. We'll tell ourselves: "I'm not smart enough/not young enough/not old enough/not pretty enough./not as good as everyone else…" This all can come quite easily. Saying something positive can be tremendously hard to do.

The Supporting Cast

When one person goes to school, a partner, or family comes along for the ride. Relationships, particularly families are like a mobile. If you change any one part, the rest has to find a new balance.. The trade off that occurs when one half of a couple, where part of the family has a big demand for some time, other people are going to have to pick up the slack. Roles shift.

For the person in school, they're about to engage in a process of major change. Aside from what one learns, there is a process that not only occupies and absorbs, you can change how you view the world and relationships. Circumstances may be such that even the partner going to school has to work. That leaves even less time to answer questions of when will you see children if they are in the picture? When will you have quality time with your partner, find energy for a sex life, or just get things like shopping?

In some ways, for the person going to school, their social world both expands and get smaller at the same time. The student is exposed to a whole new array of people undergoing the same experience. Friendships start and grow. In a shrinking availability of time, relationship with older friends may be curtailed. Any free time becomes precious.

One thought I had as I engaged in my own process of education was that if I lost what was most important to me, I had not succeeded. My allotment of "spare time," was spent with those who were paramount in my life. If you have children in their adolescence, the odds are good that if you defer that contact time, you will grow apart. The same thing can happen in relationships with partners.

Like it or not, if you have a partner in your life, they will be coming on a journey as well. You both graduate at the end of the process. In fact, your partner should probably be the one getting the graduation presents at the end of the process. They might not have the degree, but they have endured a time of higher demand as well. Continued growth as the couple is essential during the course of school. The attrition rate for relationships is staggering. Some estimate this to be as high as 70%. This often does not take into account non-traditional relationships. Are you concerned, or perhaps scared yet? The information that your relationship has markedly stacked odds of not surviving is sobering indeed.

Part of the survival planning for going to school is having contact time with your significant other's. This may mean planned dates, or family outings. A good rule for families to adopt is that most nights, plan on having dinner together. Well, spontaneity is often a casualty of this period of time. Planning your sex life is better than having no sex life at all. Look for little times, be it meeting for lunch once a week, or planning on laying in bed on a Sunday morning to read the paper together.

For the supporting cast not going to school, there will be a lot more demands on their time as well. All the mundane tasks of cooking, cleaning, washing the toilet may fall on their shoulders. It is very important for the person not going to school have a connection with their own dreams for their future. This amounts to allotting time for the non-school partner to have that connection with their own interests and dreams. This might mean that the dishes don't always get washed, the dusting doesn't get done or that meals are simple and come out of a box. It's time to come to grips with the fact that it is important to let go of some things.

·13·
Accommodations

Facts do not cease to exist because they are
ignored.
-Aldous Huxley

Different students will have a continuum of needs when they
approach the academic accommodations. Some students get
such good control of their ADD/ADHD symptoms that they require
no accommodations whatsoever. Other students may struggle
more. The answer to the question, "Is ADD/ADHD a disability?" is
definitely a matter of "Yes, No, or Maybe." The Americans with
Disabilities Act of 1990, as it pertains to ADD/ADHD defines a
"disability" as a physical or mental impairment that substantially
limits one or more "major life activities," such as learning. Just
because one has a diagnosis of ADD/ADHD, does not necessarily
mean that that individual is disabled within the meaning of ADA.
While not an attorney, there is some recent court cases regarding
the ADA, which directly relates to adults with ADD/ADHD. These
court cases expand the definition of "major life activities" to
include concentration and cognitive functions. These cases are:

· Brown v. Cox Medical Centers. (8th Cir. 2002). The court
  stated here that "ability to perform cognitive functions" is
  a major life activity.

· Gagliardo v. Connaught Laboratories, Inc. (3rd Cir. 2002).
  Here the court held that "concentrating on remembering
  (more generally, cognitive function)" are major life activities. The courts place limitations on the scope of the Act
  as well. They ruled that ADA also has its limits. The 6th
  Circuit Court ruled that the person seeking accommo-

dations under ADA, who can fully compensate, be it by use of medications, alteration and behavior, or personal practice, does not have a "disability," as defined by the ADA. In other words, if you can fully and equally address the tasks at hand, using medications, coaching, or any other means, then you do not have a disability. This has application in school's willingness to make accommodations, but also for test accommodations when taking SAT tests such as the GRE, LSAT and MCAT, ETS, the publisher SAT for the offers many options for test-takers, including assistive technology. Getting these in place will take a minimum of seven weeks. They require fairly extensive documentation. This needs to be within the last five years. For more information on the documentation criteria, go to the section for Services for Students with Disabilities; ,ETS Disability Services (1).

A first step is gaining an understanding of your own level of disability. Where do you fall down in terms of performance, despite the use of medications or behavioral techniques? Is it difficult for you to split your attention between writing notes, and listening to the lecture? Are you able to tune out distraction enough to focus on test taking?

With schools, there is good news, and bad news. Academic institutions have a continuum of willingness to provide accommodations. At the low end, some schools (largely community colleges), have been willing to grant things like separate test taking, longer time availability and other accommodations with merely a brief note from someone in a professional capacity, who states that you have ADD/ADHD. The bad news is that other institutions are quite rigorous in what they will demand for validation that you indeed do have a disability as a result of your ADD/ADHD. Merely having the diagnosis is not enough.

The Americans with Disabilities Act (ADA) and Section 504 of the Rehabilitation Act of 1973 provide for protections against discrimination and insures services. To establish that a person is covered under the ADA, the documentation must show that the disability substantially limits the students learning.

"Substantially" limits really means: to a considerable or high degree of limitation. In determining substantial limitation, the performance of the person with the impairment is compared to the performance of the average person in the general population. Additionally, the severity of the person's impairment must be measured while considering both the positive effects of coping strategies such as medication. For example, for a person who wears glasses, they might be considered "disabled" if it were not for wearing corrective lenses. If the correction to their vision is 20/20, this eliminates them from being considered "disabled" under the ADA. If a student with ADD/ADHD, who takes medication to control their symptoms and the medications manage the ADD/ADHD effectively, they would not be considered "disabled." What matters under the ADA is the actual functioning of the person. It is not what they functioning would be without the benefit of either eyeglasses or medications, or other coping strategies that the person my employee to deal with their ADD/ADHD.

The individual's performance in a major life activities must be compared to that of the average person in the general population. It is not enough to demonstrate that, for example, reading achievement is significantly below what would be expected given tested IQ. Reading must be significantly impaired as compared to an average person in the general population with scores significantly below average. Let's say a person has a legitimate difficulty with math, but has earned above-average grades in college level math courses without accommodations. They also scored above-average on the math portion of college entrance examinations without accommodations. That person would not be considered to be substantially limited with respect to the average person in the general population, even if their grades in math courses were lower than grades in other courses. When there is an extensive record of significant accomplishments in learning, and this has occurred without any accommodations for that learning, it is difficult to conclude a substantial limitation.

Let's return to the good news-bad news of accommodations in a college setting. Many schools recognize that while a person does not meet the criteria of being "substantially limited", ADD/ADHD may provide challenges to learning that are different than those faced by the non-ADD/ADHD student. The prevailing attitude for most schools seems to be one of wanting students to maximize their potential. There is a realization that the student with ADD/ADHD compensates for their difficulties by working harder to overcome the challenges created by lack of focus. A colleague of mine has a daughter who clearly has ADD/ADHD and is also exceptionally bright. He was told by a psychiatrist that she couldn't possibly have this disorder because she had excellent grades. Fortunately in the bell shaped curve of correlation with intelligence, the individual with ADD/ADHD is likely to have the benefit of higher intelligence. What was missing in this consideration of ADD/ADHD was the degree of support, and effort for her to achieve those grades. Through the course of high school her parents provided an external structure for her completing and turning in assignments. They also provided what amounted to tutoring, which allowed her to grasp the information that she had missed in class.

The bar is definitely raised when a student seeks accommodations for the three major graduate and professional school entrance exams. These are the Law School Admissions (LSAT), the Medical College Admissions Test (MCAT) and the Graduate Record Examination (GRE). In addition to documentation of the diagnosis of ADD/ADHD, these tests will require specific testing of aptitude, achievement, intelligence, and information processing. In the case of the LSAT, personality testing is required for those who claim psychiatric disorders impact their ability to take the examination. ADD/ADHD is a diagnosis which is defined in the DSM-IV, which provides the criteria for psychiatric diagnosis. The DSM-IV does not look upon ADD/ADHD is a neurological difference. It is unfortunately considered a psychiatric condition.

There is an inherent flaw in the reasoning behind these standards for granting accommodations for the LSAT, MCAT and the GRE. People applying to graduate and professional school are generally going to be accomplished students, with grade point averages that place them at the top of their class. There is no recognition that such achievement may have required efforts above and beyond that of the non-ADD/ADHD student. When a student has a high-level of achievement, the case for substantial impairment is extraordinarily difficult to prove. Taking these entrance exams really becomes playing on an uneven field. While not wanting to give some participants and undue advantage, it negates the difficulties some students having the testing environment. It is fortunate that many law, medical and graduate schools do look beyond just the numbers.

A list of the approved neuropsychiatric testing instruments appears in the appendix of this book.

Obtaining Academic Accommodations

Academic institutions vary widely in how comprehensive the validation of the need for accommodations to learning. They need to be petitioned for with the advocacy of a trained professional. On-line testing does not have the validity found in approved neuropsychiatric testing instruments. People may go to a variety of web sites and use the on-line tests. These give a good indication of ADD/ADHD, but they do pass the criteria for ADA. They are not standardized and backed by the level of examination needed to verify their validity. I may direct a person to take one of the web based tests. I do this as a screening rather than individual have to be liable for the cost

1. First, professionals need to document that they are qualified to evaluate and diagnose ADD/ADHD. Some mention that they have comprehensive training in the differential diagnosis of ADHD, and direct experience with this population. This may include psychologists, neuro-psychologist, psychiatrists, psychiatric nurse practitioners, developmental pediatricians and other relevantly trained medical professionals. The name, title and professional credentials of the evaluator should include information about license and/or certification is well as area specialization for national testing, and accommodation letter should also include the state where the professional is practicing and license numbers and how the clinician can be reached.

2. Provide a summary of educational, medical, family history and behavioral observations. ADD/ADHD must first be manifested in childhood. The difficulty is that often

that is not diagnosed in childhood. The professional must show that ADD/ADHD has presented itself in more than one setting. Relevant historical information is quite helpful. I will include things such as the person's driving record, including number of moving violations, and auto accidents.

3. The professional must provide a formal diagnosis consistent with the criteria found in the DSM-IV-TR or the ICD-9. This should include all testing, associated with providing the person with assessment using a licensed test instrument.

4. The professional should provide a detailed statement of the functional limitations related to academic performance. This may speak to the inherent problems found in a distracting environment. This is an interpretive summary of the patterns of inattentiveness, impulsivity, inattention/ hyperactivity across the life span. Document the use of medication and whether it had a positive result. Be prepared to make a statement regarding residual difficulties that are not addressed using medications. The presence of a school plan such as an Individualized Educational Plan (IEP) or a 504 plan are insufficient documentation. These can be included in records of prior accommodations. I will mirror the DSM-IV-TR when I describe this in my narrative.

5. Any alternative diagnosis and explanation for the student's problem should be addressed. This includes any co-occurring problems such as medical, psychiatric, neurological or personality disorders which may either confound the diagnosis of ADD/ADHD or intensify the impairment.

6. The professional should provide a specific list of the reasonable academic accommodations. The narrative should provide an indication as to why specific accommodations are needed and how the effects of the ADD/ADHD symptoms are mediated by the accommodations. Each accommodation that is recommended should

include a rationale. The diagnostic report must include specific recommendations for accommodations which are realistic, and that post secondary institutions can reasonably provide. This should be correlated with specific functional limitations determined through interview, observation, and/or testing. Prior documentation is often quite helpful in determining appropriate services in the past. Current documentation must validate the need for services based on the individual's present level of functioning in the educational setting. The goal is to minimize the impact of these functional limitations on the student's academic performance and participation in the program and activities of the institution.

An accommodation letter appears in the appendix of this book. This particular letter is fairly basic, but will pass muster for most colleges and universities. It will be made available to clinicians as a download from the book's website. The most comprehensive level of evaluation can be found at the ETS website and is employed when seeking accommodations for the Graduate Record Examination (1).

Academic accommodations are supposed to meet the student's disability-related needs. They are not there to functionally alter the nature of the academic program. They are also not intended to provide remediation (basic skills in the educational process such as grammar, math of English as a second language).

DSM-IV Diagnostic Criteria for ADD/ADHD

The Diagnostic and Statistical Manual of Mental Disorders is published by the American Psychiatric Association. There have been five major revisions to this manual since it was first published in 1952. The DSM-V is projected for publication in 2012. While there are many criticisms of the DSM, it provides an operational definition for diagnosis. In the case of ADD/ADHD, it looks upon this is a mental disorder, rather than a neurologic difference.

One of the prime criticisms of the DSM is its 'medicalization' of human nature. It also fails to provide any sense of context to the presence of particular symptoms. Coming from an illness model, it adds to the stigma associated with ADD/ADHD.

Parting Thoughts

It is difficult to escape the 'medicalization' of ADD/ADHD. It requires the services of a provider with a license to prescribe to be able to use medications as a tool. You're mandated to see that person periodically, even though once medications are well dialed in, little will change. The dependence on a provider if you wish to use medications is a necessary evil. Hopefully, if you do chose to use medications, your visits with your provider will be more than renewing prescriptions. I believe in taking enough time and opening the door to using that session for coaching questions. Medications are a tool which is best supported by gaining skills to surround and support use of that tool. Coaching and therapy can be of enormous benefit in putting ADD/ADHD into the proper perspective.

Realize that the map is not the territory. The definitions of ADD/ADHD are not as important as how you define yourself. It is important to see yourself not as the challenges you face but as how you face those challenges. In as much as ADD/ADHD can lead to struggles, it is also a gift. It is part you what makes you unique. It is a factor in the very different ways you are able to think and create. On the practical side, people who can think in a synthesis mode are, on average paid more than linear thinkers.

You alone have the crystal ball to know what you need or want. You need to be your own best advocate. What helps in knowing what you need is becoming knowledgeable about the challenges you face. Do what you must to educate yourself about any of life's challenges you face. Ask for support from the important people in your life. Set your sights high. The problem is not in reaching further and missing the mark but in setting your goals and aspirations too low.

Appendix A —Tools for Clinicians

I find the work I do with my ADD/ADHD client's some of my most enjoyable clinical activity. They are bright, inquisitive people and you are blessed with the ability to make often profound changes in their lives. In treating people with ADD/ADHD, you will encounter clients of clinicians, who, however well meaning, that have done sub-standard work. ADD/ADHD is both over diagnosed and under diagnosed. In the best of all worlds, we know what we know; we know what we don't know. Best of all, we know who to point a person to who can appropriately assess what is going on. None of us are without our limits. It is important to recognize these.

I believe people have a right to be informed about any new innovations in treatment and alternatives to medications. Coaching and psychotherapy have their importance. It compliments and completes the process of successful adaptation to what can be a real asset in a person's life. If you don't do coaching or psychotherapy, find good people who do. Make those referrals. Often what letters a clinician has behind their name is not an indication of their level of skill and expertise. Some of the very best coaches and therapists are trained at a Master's level and are enormously skilled and helpful to clients.

All of the following resources will be available as free downloads to clinicians on my web site: http://www.stimulusdrivenbrain.com

ETS Disability Services P.O. Box 6054 Princeton, NJ 08541-6054 USA
Monday-Friday 8:30 a.m. to 5 p.m., EST

- E-mail: stassd@ets.org
- Phone: 1-609-771-7780 1-866-387-8602
  (toll free in U.S., U.S. Territories and Canada)
- TTY: 1-609-771-7714
- Fax: 1-609-771-7165

ADD/ADHD MEDICATION LOG

Name_____

Medication(s)_____

***Rate your experience with
+ = better
- = worse
N = no change

Effects/side effects	Sun. (mo/day)	Mon.	Teu.	Wed.	Thu.	Fri.	Sat.
Dose in mg, time taken							
Duration of effect in hours							
Other med's taken							
Effect on concentration/ focus							
Effect on ability to plan/prioritize							
Effect on irritability, impatience, frustration							
Effect on Anxiety, worry							
Effect on Mood							
Effect on Impulsivity							
Effect on memory							
Effect on sleep							
Effect on relationships							
Feeling after it has worn off							

Your Letterhead

Any-City College   Date
Office of Student Services

Dear _____:

I am writing on behalf of my patient,_____ in support of his petition for educational accommodations under the Americans with Disabilities Act. The process of evaluation began with a general diagnostic intake conducted on ___Date___. This was followed by testing for ADD/ADHD using the Connor's CAARS-Self-Report: Long Version (CAARS-S:L). Mr._____ scored in the __th through __th T score for inattentive symptoms on the three subtests and the __th through __ rd T score for hyperactivity symptoms on the three subtests. Two of three measures met criteria for the diagnosis of the disorder (results > the 61st T score). Mr._____ has a diagnosis of 314.01 ADD/ADHD, Combined Type. The upper range is found for inattentive symptoms and his ADD/ADHD plays a significant role in his functioning.

Mr._____ has been diagnosed with ADD/ADHD as an adult. As part of his interview process, I utilized the CAADID developmental interview. Unfortunately we were not able to access a historical record of past grade reports, or intelligence testing. There is every indication that Mr._____ had ADD/ADHD as a child. All aspects of the developmental interview were consistent with this diagnosis. The presence of ADD/ADHD in childhood is a necessary criteria to establish a diagnosis as an adult.

We began medication trials to address his difficulties with focus. Mr._____ has had a very good response to medications. His response greatly assisted his occupational functioning. Medications, in Mr._____'s case are however not the whole answer given residual deposits not addressed by medications alone. Often environmental modifications are helpful, particularly in test taking situations, hence the request for accommodations.

ADD/ADHD can lead to difficulty with what are called executive functioning. Planning and holding events in one's mind and taking the whole apart and reconstituting are examples of this.

ADD/ADHD can also impair sense of time and lead to slow retrieval of information. Written comprehension and auditory comprehension can be compromised. The overall effect is to somewhat slow one's cognitive process. This says nothing about innate intelligence. Many people, to include Mr._____ have better than average to superior intelligence. Testing can be a poor reflection of abilities and knowledge base.

The following accommodations are requested when he takes tests and engages in the tasks of his education;

- A course synopsis for all classes detailing what papers and due and when, and what papers are due and when. Some of Mr._____ current instructors are informing student of these expectations as the quarter progresses. This does not allow Mr._____ the ability to plan for his time needs throughout the course of the quarter.
- Testing in a separate space from the larger group to decrease stimuli and distraction.
- Taking tests on an un-timed basis.
- At least two breaks of up to 20 minutes during the course of the testing interval for any test longer than 90 minutes.
- Class seating arrangement which place him in the front of the class. Frequently people with ADD/ADHD take in information if they can see the person talking (inclusive of their lips moving).
- A note taker for lecture based classes to alleviate needing to spit attention.

My professional training includes _____ I am currently licensed as a _____ in the state of _____. (License #_____). I've been in practice, as a _____ for in excess of __ years. I have in excess of ___ hours of specialized training in diagnosis and assessment of ADD/ADHD. I have in excess of __ years experience treating adults with ADD/ADHD. Further, I have a clinical appointment at _____, which is a University of _____ affiliate training Hospital.

Thank-you for your consideration of this request for testing accommodations. Should you need or wish further information regarding Mr._____ or the nature of ADD/ADHD and beneficial accommodations, please do not hesitate to call. With appropriate release of information, I would be happy to discuss this with you further. With these accommodations, Mr._____ will be able to demonstrate his abilities to their fullest.

Regards,

DEVELOPMENTAL HISTORY, ADD

1. Gestational history
2. Delivery risk factors
3. Temperament as a child.
   Excessive fussing or crying
   Resistance to being comforted
   Difficulty maintaining sleeping + eating schedules
   Excessive running, jumping
   Overly aggressive, overly withdrawn
   Poor sibling relationships
4. Grade school/ Middle school
   Poor grades
   Fidgeting
   Poor attention in class
   Interrupting, blurting out
   Becoming emotional easily
   Noncompliance with rules
   Delayed social skills
   Retention in grade
5. High school
   Poor or inconsistent grades
   Chronic low self esteem
   Difficulty with authority figures
   Excessive risk taking
   Early drug/ ETOH use
   Continued peer problems
   Poorly organized
   Low productivity in school
6. College performance.
7. Occupational History
8. Relationship history

Issues of self esteem, where do you find you fall down

ADD: Mom's Remembering Infancy Questionnaire

Was your child "overactive in the womb?"

Did your child have any developmental delays i.e. slow to walk, to talk to stand or sit up?

Did your child have difficulty establishing an eating or sleeping pattern?

Did your child have any problem getting along with peers as a toddler?

Did your child frequently fight with their siblings?

Did preschool or early teachers complain you child was noisy or disruptive?

Did later teachers ever write "Not working up to full potential"?

(An e-mail sent with directions and appointment time to all new patients. I now use an on-line appointment service. It saves huge amounts of time trying to reach people by phone and gives the client four e-mail reminders of their upcoming appointment.)

Information for People Seeking Treatment for ADD/ADHD

A little bit about the process:
The starting point for all of my clients is a 90-minute intake interview. ADD/ADHD is characterized by what are called co-morbidities, a fancy way of saying other issues going on at the same time. These can be depression, anxiety disorders or bipolarity spectrum disorders. These need to be stabilized before we can treat potential ADD/ADHD.

At the first meeting, you will be given testing to further assess ADD/ADHD. If you have a significant other in your life, they will fill out an observer form. I discourage people from looking to on-line tests as they are not well standardized and at best give an indication. The testing I use is a 'gold standard' testing instrument. When we have our next appointment, per your wishes, your significant other is welcome to come to the next session. I'll leave time for the education/questions part but our goal is to start on medications if they are indicated. Realize that everyone has some symptoms. It is just as important to have it correctly diagnosed even if you don't meet criteria for the diagnosis. ADD/ADHD is both over diagnosed and under diagnosed. It's important to get it right.

If you have been previously diagnosed, then I would like to see previous records, if they are available. I will often re-test, particularly if someone was treated as a child but not treated recently treated. For some people, the symptoms lessen and medications may not be indicated. I also take a bio-behavioral approach to treatment. Sometimes coaching, either with myself or others who do ADD/ADHD coaching is quite helpful.

I need to charge for testing. Sometime insurance will pick up most of the charges for this, sometimes it will not. I try to keep this reasonable and charge $_____ for testing. We'll first bill your insurance. If it doesn't not cover my fee, then my billing person will bill you for this amount.

I ask people to become informed about ADD/ADHD. I suggest some very good books, which are good standards for giving an overview to ADD and treatment. They are as follows:

Out of the Fog
Treatment Options and Coping Strategies for Adult Attention Deficit Disorder by Kevin R. Murphy and Suzanne Levert

Driven to Distraction
By Edward Hallowell and John J. Ratey

Is It You, Me or Adult ADD?
Stopping the Roller Coaster When Someone You Love has Attention Deficit Disorder by Gina Pera and Russell Barkley

ADD and Romance
by Jonathan Halverstadt

Doing this work has many restrictions. These include the inability to call in or fax new prescriptions and the inability to do refills. When dose is established and you move to quarterly follow-up, you will get three identical prescriptions. If you lost a prescription or you fail to make an appointment prior to running out I will of medications I will need to charge you a small fee for their replacement. For me, this process included, looking up you medications and DOB, writing the prescription, documenting in your chart, and mailing or having out for pick-up. This all takes time.

I look forward to working with you. Often addressing one's ADD/ADHD can result in life changing differences in the way people function. In many ways, it is a gift in that it often neurological difference, it can result in difficulty with how you perceive yourself. I started my career with formal training as a therapist. Short-term talk orient work can often be helpful as well. We'll talk about what you feel you need when we meet. My perspective is one of viewing medications as a tool but rarely the whole answer.

Regards,

(I send this as an e-mail attachment to all new ADD/ADHD clients)

Prior Authorization Plan Liability Attachment

Dear Health Plan Drug Prior Authorization Review Staff;

Health Plan Name or Company_____.

Attached is a prescription drug prior authorization request for one of my patients who has prescription drug benefit coverage through your organization. If you disagree with my medical recommendations to treat:

_____ (Name of Patient) with
_____ (name of drug), please sign this letter and return a copy for my files.

If my request is denied, your signature indicates that you are now making a medical decision that affects my patient, and in this case, your decision is against my medical recommendation. Your signature therefore indicates that you will accept responsibility for any adverse outcome. (Many states now allow managed care patients to seek compensation from their managed care organization for adverse outcomes as a result of managed care medical management decisions.)

Thank you for your attention to this matter.

_____.

Health Plan's or Acting Agent's signature

_____.

Health Plan's or Acting Agents Printed Name

Date of Signature:_____

Regards,

_____.

Signature of Professional

*Author's note: I like to find the companies legal department and mail a copy of this letter to them as well.

Appendix B

Sources

Chapters 1 and 2

1. Beck, Aaron T. Cognitive Therapy and Emotional Disorders, International Universities Press Inc., 1975 ISBN 0-8236-0990-1

2. Ellis, Albert. Rational Emotive Behavior Therapy: A Therapist's Guide (2nd Edition), with Catharine MacLaren. Impact Publishers, 2005. ISBN 1-886230-61-7.

3. Hartman, Thom: Beyond ADD. Underwood Books.1996 ISBN 1-887424-12-1.

4. Diagnostic and Statistical Manual of Mental Disorders (Fourth edition---text revision (DSM-IV-TR). Washington, DC: American Psychiatric Association. 2000

5. I. K. Berg, "Family based services: A solution-focused approach." New York: Norton. 1994.

Chapter 3

1. Kessler, R.C., Avenevoli, S., Greif Green, J., Gruber, M.J., Heeringa, S., Guyer, M., He, Y., Jin, R., Kaufman, J., Merikangas, K.R., Sampson, N.A., Zaslavsky, A.M. (in press). The National Comorbidity Survey Adolescent Supplement (NCS-A): III. Concordance of DSM-IV/CIDI diagnoses with clinical reassessments. Journal of the American Academy of Child and Adolescent Psychiatry 48(4), 386-399.

2. Reuben, D. Saving Primary Care. The American Journal of Medicine, Volume 120, Issue 1, Pages 99-102.

3. Jasinski, J.R., Krishnan, S., Human Pharmacology of Intravenous Lisdexamphetamine Dimesylate: Abuse Liability in Adult Stimulant Users. Journal of Psychopharmacology 2008

Chapter 4

1. Amen, Daniel Images of Human Behavior: A Brain SPECT Atlas Mindworks Press . 2004

2. HealthNewsDigest.com. Vyvanse CII Provided Significant Efficacy at 14 Hours After Administration in Adults with ADHD Jul 6, 2009 - 4:53:05 PM

Chapter 5

1. Spencer TJ. Depressive disorders and ADHD. Program and abstracts of the 154th Annual Meeting of the American Psychiatric Association; May 5-10, 2001; New Orleans, Louisiana. Industry Symposium 46C

2. Biederman J, Faraone SV, Keenan K, et al. Further evidence for family- genetic risk factors in attention deficit disorder: patterns of comorbidity in probands and relatives in psychiatrically and pediatrically referred samples. Arch Gen Psychiatry. 1992;49:728-738.

3. Nierenberg, S. Miyahara, T. Spencer, S. Wisniewski, M. Otto, N. Simon, M. Pollack, M. Ostacher, L. Yan, R. Siegel Clinical and Diagnostic Implications of Lifetime Attention-Deficit/Hyperactivity Disorder Comorbidity in Adults with Bipolar Disorder: Data from the First 1000 STEP-BD Participants Biological Psychiatry, Volume 57, Issue 11, Pages 1467-1477

Chapter 10

1. Jacobson, E. (1938). Progressive Relaxation. Chicago: University of Chicago Press

Chapter 13

1. Gardner, Howard. Intelligence Reframed: Multiple Intelligences for the 21st Century. Basic Books, 1999

Chapter 14

1. Educational Testing Service. Policy Statement for Documentation of Attention-Deficit/Hyperactivity Disorder (ADHD) in Adolescents and Adults, 2nd Edition, 2008

Index

X, Y, Z

about the author

George H. Glade, M.C., M.N.,
ARNP. Mr. Glade has a diverse
clinical practice encompassing
work in the psychiatric emergency
room of Seattle's major trauma
center as well as private practice.
He has a clinical appointment
at the University of Washington/
Harborview Medical Center. His
professional areas of interest
are varied and include maternal
depression, bipolarity, ADD/ADHD
and head injury. He is a highly
entertaining speaker for professionals, the business community
and the public. His own stimulus
driven brain finds interest in writing fiction, fishing hiking, painting,
rowing and traveling in Central and
South America.

Contact: *Mr. Glade can be contacted for speaking engagements through
5550 Angstrom Press, LLC at PubSDB@gmail.com*

Notes

Notes

Notes

A FREE offer from the Author of The Stimulus Driven Brain.

Join my mailing list whether you purchase the book or not! You can even let your friend's in on this free offer, all for just for the effort of joining my e-mail ist. Every month I will be sending you different ways of maximizing your success in school and in life. Join me in what is a mission of both education and empowerment.

If you are a clinician, I'll be doing presentations with up to the minute, evidenced based, clinical information as well as tools you can use in your practice. At my web site, I have a variety of forms, letters and other tools that I want to share with you as a way of supporting you in the valuable work that you do.

It's all found at:

Stimulusdrivenbrain.com

To order the book:
call our 24 hour toll free line at 1-800-431-1579